THE 10
COMMANDMENTS
OF WINNING
TEAMMATES

Sean Glaze

OAKWIND
BOOKS

The 10 Commandments of Winning Teammates

Copyright 2016 © Sean Glaze

This book may be ordered through booksellers or by contacting:

Oakwind Books

ISBN: 978-0-9962458-3-8 (Paperback)

ISBN: 978-0-9962458-4-5 (Digital)

Printed in the United States of America

Book arrangement: Jennifer FitzGerald - www.MotherSpider.com

DEDICATION:

To the many young men and women I had the honor to coach who worked hard to be winning teammates.

This book is a grateful nod to the impact you had on me and on the groups that you were an extraordinary part of…

"Sean is a master at telling stories... and this book isn't just a story. It's a collection of incredible stories within a story — each one enjoyable and encapsulating a transformational truth that will help you be someone's 'best teammate ever.'"

- Kevin Monroe, Executive Coach and Founding Steward of Living Your WHY

"...this road trip that Nick Turner takes is a real game changer. The 10 Commandments of Winning Teammates will force you to look at your own life and in so doing, will point out that anyone's journey will improve by adhering to these ten powerful principles."

- Bob Rathbun, Atlanta Hawks TV Broadcaster and Keynote Speaker.

"Ten terrific reminders make this a must read for anyone who works with others. Grab a copy for your whole department! You will be more profitable and more productive!"

- Jill Lublin, International speaker and 3x Best selling author

"You not only take a journey with the main character Nick, but you take a personal journey into your own past of success and mistakes. I highly recommend reading "The Ten Commandments of a Winning Teammate" no matter what business or sports field you may be in."
- Lewis Preston, NCAA D1 Basketball Coach, Speaker & Consultant

"A small book with a huge impact! Sean Glaze's Ten Commandments of Winning Teammates is a fictional story with a collection of real insights about how you can be a more effective team member. I encourage anyone working on or leading a team to read this. It will make you more aware of the impact your questions and behaviors have on others, and you'll learn what you can do to make your organization more successful. These are valuable insights you can put into practice immediately."
- Mike Figliuolo, Managing Director of thoughtLEADERS, LLC and author of One Piece of Paper, The Elegant Pitch, and Lead Inside the Box

Contact Sean

To Book Sean for Your Next Corporate Event,
Visit Him Online at:

WWW.GREATRESULTSTEAMBUILDING.COM

CONTENTS

THE 10 COMMANDMENTS OF WINNING TEAMMATES

Vital Lessons for Improving Your Value - Because Team Success Requires More Than Technical Talent

The Ten Commandments of
Winning Teammates

1 - Remember to <u>have fun</u> and remain positive

2 - Always give and request <u>clear expectations</u>

3 - Frequently <u>share appreciation</u> and thanks

4 - Continue to grow and <u>stay coachable</u>

5 - Be aware of and <u>encourage others</u>

6 - <u>Do more than is expected</u> with enthusiasm

7 - <u>Respect the clock</u> and the calendar

8 - <u>Know your role</u> and contribute your strengths

9 - <u>Prioritize team goals</u> ahead of personal gains

10 - Claim personal <u>responsibility for results</u>

PREFACE

how this book will make you more successful

I learned a lot from coaching basketball over the last 20 years.

I first focused on learning the X's and O's of the game, and the importance of putting people in positions where they could take advantage of their strengths.

And it was only later that I learned the importance of inspiring people to lead from where they are, which I discussed in my book *The Unexpected Leader* – and the importance of building and maintaining a positive culture, which I discussed in my book *Rapid Teamwork*.

But I also learned the importance of having strong teammates if you want your team to succeed over time.

When I transitioned to working with corporate groups as a team building event facilitator and conference speaker, I was impressed by how similar their challenges were to the ones that I had experienced as a high school basketball coach.

In working with organizations across the country, whether it was school faculties, sales teams, medical office staff, or a team from any other industry, I found that good talent and strategy was essential — but never sufficient.

And while being a winning teammate does not mean you will always be on a championship team, I would argue that every championship team always has its fair share of winning teammates...

When my son began playing, I shared with him the same message that my daughters had heard from me when they first dabbled in athletics. I said that I had no idea if they would ever be the most talented kid on their team, but that I was never going to be a parent who cared about points or rebounds or the accolades that came with being seen as a great player.

Instead, what I told them I would ALWAYS care about is that they work hard enough to be seen as a great teammate.

At the time, my definition of being a great teammate for my children (who were probably around 6 or 8 years old) was simple. I told them that they should always play hard, they should always listen to their coach, and they should always care about and encourage the other kids on their team.

For them, that just meant to run instead of walking, it meant having hungry eyes and ears when the coach was talking at practices and during games, and it meant getting up to high five and clap for the good kids when they came off the court.

Well, those simple expectations grew over time − but the foundational thought has remained simple and never lost its significance. You may not always be an impressive talent on your team, but with the right attitude and effort you can always be an impressive teammate.

This applies to YOU because it isn't only relevant in basketball or athletics.

The truth is that in most organizations, **people are hired for their skill and expertise and then fired for their attitudes and behaviors**.

The world that many of us grew up in, where Clint Eastwood and John Wayne movies taught that toughness meant doing everything by ourselves as isolated renegades, has slowly disappeared.

Today, the people who succeed and advance

are those who <u>understand the importance of interpersonal relations and collaboration</u>.

Today, people need talented teammates.

But toxic talent will eventually sabotage a team's performance.

And it isn't just in locker rooms that this holds true...

According to a 2015 article in the Washington Post, Deloitte simplified their own employee evaluation process by scrapping the standard assessment they had used for years and rewriting it to include only four simple questions.

The first two are answered on a five-point scale, from "strongly agree" to "strongly disagree;" the second two have yes or no options:

1. *Given what I know of this person's performance, and if it were my money, I would award this person the highest possible compensation increase and bonus.*

2. *Given what I know of this person's performance, I would always want him or her on my team.*

3. *This person is at risk for low performance.*

4. *This person is ready for promotion today.*

And that is all they focus on.

Of course, the major shift is in including <u>question number two</u>. Corporations and their consulting firms are now aware of the incredible impact that good (or bad) teammates have on organizational culture.

And no matter how talented you are at your job, this book is relevant to you!

Why...?

Because success is about the repetition of fundamentals.

For exceptionally talented readers, this book highlights the fundamental skills that you need to acquire in order to thrive where you are and continue to grow.

Without the focus on being a winning teammate, toxic talent becomes less and less valued – and behaviors that might be tolerated for a brief time early on will eventually become unacceptable and lead to unexpected issues.

And for normal people, just working to build a reputation as a solid contributor, a focus on the fundamental interpersonal lessons in this book will significantly improve your standing as a more valuable member of the team you serve.

Whether it is in basketball or business, being a winning teammate means becoming a small contributing part of something more significant than yourself.

I think you will enjoy the story and the lessons it shares.

More importantly, you will enjoy the

impact that it has on your own personal and professional success when you apply the lessons in your life.

CHAPTER 1

look ahead with better questions

They knocked on the door at 9:14 am.

Nick was holding a large Styrofoam cup, half full of Dunkin Donuts coffee. His coffee maker and mugs had already been packed into one of the cardboard boxes.

Nick maneuvered around the obstacle course of furniture and boxes, stacked like a maze of oversized Lego towers, to get to the front door of the second floor apartment he was leaving.

Through the peep hole, he saw two large men standing outside, one glancing down at a clipboard. They both had on a green t-shirt with the company logo and khaki shorts.

It was the movers.

Nick opened the door. "Morning, fellas. Which one of you is Jack?"

The one with the clipboard spoke without looking up, reading his name from the printed form in his hand. "Morning, Mister Turner — I'm Jack. We spoke on the phone last week. This is my partner, Rich. Sorry we're a few minutes late. Everything ready?"

Nick opened the door wide and motioned with his palm up to reveal his preparatory packing efforts.

"I've got a few things left to go through in the back bedroom, but the big stuff I need you guys to take is out here. I want to be out by noon, if possible."

"Yes, sir. Shouldn't be a problem. Glad you chose us to help you with your move." The guy looked up at Nick with a genuine smile. "Shouldn't take more than a couple of hours, 'less you're hiding a piano somewhere…"

Nick chuckled, and was struck by the great attitude the mover seemed to have.

"Okay…" He held up his coffee and turned to walk down the hallway. "Let me know if you need anything else — I'll be back here filling up the last few boxes I'm taking with me."

"Thanks Mister Turner. We'll get started out here then."

As he walked to the back of the apartment,

Nick heard Jack set his steel clipboard down on the granite kitchen countertop and give a few directions to his partner.

The back bedroom's closet door was still opened wide, and Nick sat down on the grey carpeted floor to survey the last bit of packing that he had to finish.

This was the collection of old stuff that he had held onto from his past that got shoved in the spare room. He should have gone through it the last time he moved, and could probably throw at least half of it away without ever missing it.

The closet shelves held a collection of flimsy shoe boxes and large plastic storage containers that protected mementos from his youth.

Baseball cards. Newspaper clippings. Old shirts and baseball caps. Plaques and trophies. The flotsam that people collect over time and struggle to part with until years later we recognize they are little more than forgotten souvenirs that take up needed space in our lives.

On his left, Nick folded open a cardboard box, and wrote "school stuff" in red sharpie.

Then beside him, on the right, he pulled open a black heavy-duty garbage bag from the roll he had purchased a few days earlier. Now he had a place for things to keep, and a place for things to trash.

He finished the last gulp of coffee, took a deep breath, and thoughtfully considered his situation.

Moving again was definitely not a fun experience.

He had always enjoyed the calls from headhunters. His education and test scores and talent had placed him on all the right lists. But while his first two jobs had started out full of promise and opportunity, they ended up essentially the same way.

"I just don't think you are a good fit for our culture…" Donna had said. Donna was the HR lady who had greeted him so enthusiastically only seven months earlier.

And now he was doing it again. Starting another job with a new boss and an HR department that was full of enthusiasm for his arrival.

But he knew that if it was going to end differently this time, he would have to do something differently.

He just didn't know what.

The storage containers he still needed to go through contained stuff from his time in high school and college, and he tossed most of it without a thought, deciding it was not important enough to earn a spot in the back of his Explorer for the trip.

Five minutes later, the small cardboard box

he had planned to use for "school stuff" was still half empty... and the black bag was filling up.

Nick had kept his high school diploma and college degrees, along with a pair of cheap sunglasses he had bought on a trip to the beach with his friends and a couple of other silly pictures and knick-knacks that made him smile... but most of the papers and other things he had believed were important enough to hold onto years ago now just seemed unnecessary.

One of the last containers he had to go through had stuff that he had collected when he played high school basketball.

He sighed and shook his head.

They could have been a pretty good team his senior year. Had talent. He had definitely worked hard to be one of the best shooters in the region. But things just hadn't clicked for them. Instead of finishing first in their area, they had finished fifth and lost the first game of the playoffs.

He didn't remember the scores – but he did remember the feelings.

His team always seemed disappointed in him, even though he shot over 40% from three that year. But Coach Watkins, and Jimmy, were two people that made him feel good about all the work he put in.

They had not been a very close team. Nick

barely got to know most of the young guys he had played with — and he hadn't spoken to Jimmy, his only real friend on the team, in over two years.

So Nick opened up the last plastic container, curious to find out if it held a few things he couldn't go to Baltimore without.

He immediately threw out the certificate of participation. Then he threw out his old practice jersey and shoes. Why had he kept those?

He put a plaque for best shooting percentage in the "keep" box next to his graduation tassel, and smiled a moment as he read through a statistics printout from his senior year of basketball.

He decided to keep that, too.

Then he threw away the playoff game program from his last game and kept a picture of his team from their last banquet.

Nick was surprised to find a brown piece of paper rolled up with a string around it.

It looked like a scroll, but it had been made with paper that looked older than it really was. When he unrolled it, he faintly recalled what it had been.

Coach Watkins, at their end of season banquet, had given one to each player — and prior to giving out the team awards he remembered something in his speech about them being just as important off the court as they were on the court.

But everybody had gotten the same thing – a list of rules - so Nick hadn't even opened it up to read what it said. He didn't need rules anymore. He was through with basketball at that point.

So here it was again. Opened, finally. And he read it with a wry smile.

At the top, in bold green letters, it said: **"The 10 Commandments of Winning Teammates."**

Beneath that title was a list of ten things that Coach Watkins had probably talked a lot about during the season. But Nick hadn't paid much attention when he was a player. He was just there to make shots and win games.

Before his eyes were able to glance down to skim over the list of rules, though, Nick's phone rang. On the screen, he saw it was his sister.

"This should be fun," he thought to himself.

"Hey, sis. What's up?"

"Just thought you'd want to know about dad. He's not doing well, Nick. Are you gonna be able to help us out over the next few days?"

"Abbie… you know I've got the new job starting… I'm elbow deep in boxes and moving. This just isn't a good time. Can you hold down the fort a while longer for me? Promise I'll try to get there to see him in a couple of weeks."

The other end was silent, but breathing.

"Okay?"

"Nick, I can't believe... I mean, it's always the same thing with you... You know what, don't worry about it. Eric and I will handle it."

"Abbie... I really am sorry. Come on... I'll get over there after I'm settled to give you guys a break. Raleigh is the same distance from Baltimore that it is from Atlanta..."

More silence.

"Come on. I'll only be five or six hours away. I'll come see him. Just gimme a week or two."

Nick was still holding the scroll in his other hand, but it had rolled back up so he couldn't read the list while he waited for his sister's anger to pass.

"Just..." She took a deep breath. "Drive safe, little brother. I hope things work out better for you up there... But dad isn't doing well. Okay?"

"Okay. Got it. Really. I'll call you, Okay?"

"Sure. Alright. Bye, Nick."

"Bye Abs"

He put down the phone and looked again at the scroll, holding it open and flattening it against the floor with his right hand.

The 10 Commandments of Winning Teammates.

Nick's eyes scanned the list and he began to recall his coach's voice, stern and demanding, bubble out of the past and into his ears.

Coach Watkins loved his catchy sayings. The guys sometimes used to joke that he should have been a preacher...

Wow... Nick hadn't spoken to Coach Watkins since he got the call to congratulate him on his college graduation. That was three years ago.

Maybe coach was at the same number? Nick thought it might be fun to give him a call to let him know that his gift was finally getting opened.

He left the paper there on the floor beside him to roll back up, and looked through his phone contacts for Coach Watkins, then pressed the call button.

It rang twice, then Nick heard Coach Watkins' deep, raspy voice.

"Yeah? What can I do for you?"

"Coach Watkins! Wow – its Nick. Nick Turner."

"Well... hello there Nicky! What are you up to these days?"

"Hey Coach. Just wanted to give you a call. Thought you'd like to know I finally opened up your gift from our banquet!"

"What gift was that?"

"You know — the scroll. The old brown paper you printed out and rolled up with the winning teammate rules on it. I just found it going through my old school stuff!"

"Ha… well that's interesting. So you are just now opening it?"

"Yes, sir. Getting ready to move to Baltimore for a new job, and I had it in one of my boxes. Just thought you'd like to know I still have it."

"I'm glad you do, Nicky… But I guess it hasn't done you much good there in that box!"

"Ha… no sir. Guess not."

"So how are things? Moving to Baltimore, huh?"

"Yes sir. Leaving Atlanta today, actually. Gonna make the drive up with a few things, and my stuff will join me up there tomorrow."

"So what's been going on with your team in Atlanta? What's taking you to Baltimore?"

"Aw… just not a good fit, I guess. I think the job up in Baltimore will be better."

"Why is that, Nicky?"

"I don't know. Just looking for something different I guess. Not everyone there at my old job was the easiest to work with, you know?"

"Well, I… I think it's funny you would say it that way."

Nicky caught himself… he knew what Coach was talking about. His senior year he had complained a bit about the younger guys not being easy to work with on the court.

"Okay, Coach. Well, I just wanted to let you know I appreciate everything. Hope you are doing well…"

"Wait a second, Nicky. Before you go. Maybe it's a good thing you called."

"Sir?"

"Well, I mean, I think it's a good thing you found that paper I gave you. I think maybe you need it more than you think…"

"Why do you say that, Coach?"

"Let me ask you a question, Nicky. Who is the best teammate you ever had?"

Nick was surprised at the question, but then he was challenged by it. He had a hard time thinking of anybody that fit that description.

"I guess I'm not sure, Coach. I kinda always did stuff myself. Never wanted to be needy, so guess I've been more of a lone wolf…"

"Doesn't have to be as a player, only. Could be at work, too. Anybody pop into your mind?"

"Never noticed. Guess I really never thought about it. I mean, Jimmy was the guy I was closest to back on our team… guess he was a good teammate."

"But because you were focused on your job – as a player or as an employee – you never asked yourself what it meant to be a winning teammate?"

17

"Guess not, Coach."

"You know, Nick — your experience at your last job may be a lot like what you experienced as a player."

"What do you mean, Coach?"

"Well, I mean that being a winning teammate is more than just wearing the same uniform or being in the same office. Being a better teammate — having a better life - starts with asking better questions of yourself... and others. Since you have the list with you, I'd like for you to try something..."

"What's that?" Nick wasn't going to commit to anything, but it would be interesting to at least hear what Watkins was going to suggest.

"Well, first, I'm not going to make you memorize the list. It's important, but you'll see that for yourself if you try this idea I'm going to suggest. I think will be good for you."

"Okay... what is it?"

"Nicky — one of my favorite quotes when I heard Coach Bobby Knight speak at a clinic was 'everybody looks, but not everybody sees.' What he meant is that you see and appreciate only what you look for. If you look for excuses and problems, you see those... but look for examples of positive teammates, and you see those too."

Coach Watkins paused a moment to let

that sink in before he shared his idea.

"What I want you to try will help you to see better. But it's like a drill in basketball - you have to actually do it… saying you will do it and actually taking action are two very different things. But what I'm going to suggest, you don't have to do for months to see improvement. You only have to do it for 24 hours to see it working."

"Okay, Coach. I'll try it… for you. So what is it?" He was curious now.

"Well, Nicky – Here it is…. I want you to ask one question of each person you interact with for the next 24 hours. Just one question. Can you do that?"

"I could. Kinda depends on the question, Coach. What is it?"

"You have the paper with you now. It really is a helpful list. And I want you to keep it with you. And what I want you to ask the people you meet is this: 'Who is the best teammate you have ever had?'"

"That's it?" Nick was surprised. He expected something more substantial.

"That's it. But you will be surprised how much better it will help you see yourself and the people around you. But you have to ask everybody that you talk with, got it?"

"Got it, Coach."

"And you are going to do it?"

This was really a much more awkward conversation that he had anticipated. He just wanted to say hello and let Coach know he had found the paper…

"Yeah, Coach. I'll do it."

"Promise?"

"Yes, sir. Really."

"Good, Nicky. Give me a call back after you're settled in Baltimore. I'll want to hear how it goes for you, okay?"

"Yes, sir. Good talking with you, Coach."

"You too, Nicky. Just remember to ask the question. Better questions lead to better eyes."

"You got it, Coach. I'll call you in a couple of days."

"You better! Well, have a safe trip…"

"Yes, sir. Goodbye, Coach."

"Bye, Nicky."

Nick put his phone on the floor and looked again at the list of 10 Commandments.

Asking a stranger about who they remember as the best teammate they ever had seemed silly.

But he had promised.

And it couldn't hurt, right?

After an underachieving senior year… and after leaving two jobs in the last three years… maybe this was a chance for him to be more coachable.

Maybe asking a different question would help him to see something different.

Nick tossed the empty coffee cup into the black bag and slid his phone in his front pocket. After one more quick look at it, he put the scroll from coach in the cardboard box of school items and closed it, then stood up.

He needed to take out the trash, then he needed to get on the road.

Baltimore was waiting.

CHAPTER 2

remember to have fun and remain positive

Nick walked out of the bedroom with a half-filled trash bag in his hand and noticed the two moving men laughing together as they carried out his living room armoire.

The armoire was the heaviest piece of furniture he owned, and he had said more than a few bad words when he spent almost an hour moving it from one side of the room to another over a year ago.

That left a dozen or so large boxes left in the living room, along with some pictures and the couch and bookcase. It looked like they had gotten most everything else to the truck.

Nick carried the bag outside to place it beside his Explorer. He could drop it in the dumpster on the way out later…

In the parking lot, he saw the movers stepping out of their truck.

Jack patted the armoire, which was already secured to the passenger side wall, and smiled at him. "She was a heavy one!"

"Yeah… looks like you guys have done this once or twice, though." Nick replied.

"Ha… yep. We've seen a few tough armoires or couches or dressers over the years."

"So how long have you been in the moving business?"

Jack looked at Rich, as if to get confirmation. "Maybe 8 years now? Sound about right, Rich?"

Rich laughed. "Man. That means you're getting old. Good thing you've got me to handle the heavy stuff."

Nick hesitated. He had made a promise, and he might as well follow through on it – even if it did feel a bit weird.

"Okay… so I want to ask you guys a question."

"Yeah? Shoot!" Rich said.

"I uh… doing stuff like this… moving, I mean… your day depends a lot on the person you are working with, right?"

"Absolutely" Jack said.

Nick continued, afraid to break his momentum.

"So, who is the best teammate you have ever had?"

Rich spoke up first.

"Definitely this guy." He pointed at Jack. "He's the reason we started this business!"

Jack flashed a modest grin.

Nick looked on interestedly as he explained.

"You see," Rich continued, "we've only been working together in this company for the last two years. Before that, we worked for a different company. And it was nowhere near as much fun."

"Really? What do you mean?" Nick asked, curious.

"Jack and I were just employees at a larger moving business. But it didn't feel the same way getting up to go to work each day.

Jack interrupted with agreement. "I hated it. I was looking for something different, because my wife couldn't stand me coming home so negative and tired."

The three men walked back inside the apartment and stood there amid the remaining boxes and pictures and furniture, talking.

When Jack paused, Rich started again to fill in the gaps. "We were both unhappy there. Most of the people we worked with were always complaining. You'd get in the truck to go to a job, and they'd just suck the energy out of you. I asked to change partners twice before I got paired up with Jack. And that was the best thing that ever happened to us."

Jack spoke again: "After that first job together, I didn't want to work with anybody else.

"Yeah," Rich said. "He actually smiled - and meant it when he said 'good morning!'"

"I went home," Jack said, "and my wife asked me what was different. And I told her – it was just the new guy I was working with. He made it fun!"

Nick leaned against the kitchen wall and nodded as they spoke. It was energizing to see their faces light up as they recalled their first days together.

"So you guys decided to leave and start your own company, huh?"

"Not at first," Jack answered.

"Nah… Jack took a while to come around," Rich continued. "But after working together on a couple of jobs, it just got tougher and tougher to work with other people when they kept being so negative. They'd complain that we 'had to' do this or 'had to' do that. And I felt like that was wrong. Heck, I want to work with somebody who is thinking that we 'get to' do stuff. It's amazing how much different your day is when you work with people who have fun and stay positive…"

"So that is why he is the best teammate you ever had?" Nick asked.

"Yep," Rich replied. He was taking off his gloves as he talked. "Without a doubt. Jack makes something that most people see as monotonous and boring seem enjoyable. He could be doing anything, and he'd find a way to enjoy it and make the people around him enjoy it, too."

He gave a sincere nod to Jack in appreciation.

"It's not the job that's boring or difficult. That's what Jack taught me. It's the person. Don't matter if you're a mover or a mailman or answering calls all day — having fun and being positive is a choice you make. That's what makes him a good teammate."

Nick saw Jack was a bit uncomfortable with the praise his partner was sharing.

"Bet he'd say the same thing about you, huh?" Nick asked.

"I hope so," Rich said.

"Definitely." Jack answered. "You do a lot of the same stuff most every day — but the person you work with — and the attitude they bring — that's what really makes it a good or bad day."

"So, what do you think made those other people you worked with so negative?" Nick asked them both.

Rich and Jack were silent for a few moments, thinking. Then Rich walked over to a large picture that was beside the couch waiting to be put in the truck.

"It's like this picture," Rich said. "Everything is like this picture."

Both Jack and Nick waited for his explanation.

"I mean it. See, you take the frame for granted, but it is very important. I had a girl-friend who worked at an art gallery — and she told me that how you frame a painting has a lot to do with how people see it."

Rich was pointing to the thick wooden frame he was holding for emphasis. "You can take the same picture, and put it in a thick, dark, black frame — and it becomes much darker. But you can also put it inside a brighter frame. It's the way you frame the picture that makes all the difference. Some people just put a dark frame around the stuff that happens to them. Jack doesn't."

Surprisingly, that made a lot of sense, Nick thought.

Jack chimed in again. "It was a few months before I got up the courage to jump and go into business with him — and that was because my wife told me that I'd be crazy not to."

"Best decision you ever made, buddy" Rich said, pointing at him and then laughing.

"That is true," Jack confirmed.

"There's lots of people in this world," Rich concluded, "who don't have to change their job to be happier - they just have to change their frame and their attitude."

"And if they don't change their attitude," Jack added, "somebody else will change who they're working with!"

Just then Nick's phone buzzed silently. "Thanks, guys!" Nick said. "This is my sister. Better see what she needs..." and he walked back toward the bedroom again.

"Alright, then. Break time is over, pal!" Jack said. He patted the couch. "Let's get this stuff loaded up."

"You take the heavy end this time!" Rich said, smiling.

"Wow... thought you'd want to be nice to best teammate you ever had!"

Rich groaned. "Aw, man. That's gonna come back and haunt me, isn't it?"

"Definitely!" Jack joked. And they grabbed the couch to carry it out to the truck.

Nick was still in the hallway when he looked down at the text message his sister had sent him.

"Get here next week or sooner if you can. Drive safe, little brother."

His sister just wouldn't leave him alone!

Nick put the phone back in his front pocket and thought about the conversation he had just had with the movers.

He sat back down on the grey carpet beside the cardboard box he had filled.

He reached inside to grab the rolled-up piece of paper that his coach had given him nearly eight years earlier.

And it was just like he thought. The first commandment of being a winning teammate!

Was that a coincidence?

He read the paper, and sure enough, it was first on the list. He needed to talk with coach. This was weird.

And then he thought about himself and his past behavior.

Had he been more like Jack or more like the other people – the ones that Rich wanted to get away from because they complained a lot?

He had complained.

Nick thought he should call Wayne to find out what others thought of him at his last job. It's tough to see the label from inside the jar, right?

And what about basketball? He knew that

he hadn't been much fun to be around his senior year. He showed up, practiced hard, made his shots, and then left. He didn't remember laughing much with his team.

Maybe Rich was right. When it isn't fun, people don't want to be there.

And maybe, Nick thought, he had been carrying around his own dark frame.

He had probably frowned more than he smiled. He had probably been negative more than he joked.

And not just at his last job.

At his first job. And as a basketball player, too.

Teammates want the same thing, whether it is in business or in basketball.

They want to work with somebody who has energy. Who stays positive. Who makes it fun for others because of how they choose to act and talk and think.

Nick was glad he had asked them the question, and was more convinced than he expected that asking others would be a fun experience, too.

He'd wait to call coach later. He had to get on the road.

Nick grabbed two boxes and carried them out of the bedroom to load his Explorer.

CHAPTER 3

always give and request clear expectations

By noon, Nick's Explorer was filled with clothes and boxes and ready for the trip.

He had already carried the trash bags to the community dumpster, and was now waiting for the movers to empty the apartment.

It was just after 11:30 when Jack left his partner to finish loading the last few boxes and walked over with his clipboard to talk.

"Okay, Mister Turner — looks like we've just about got it!"

"Terrific," Nick answered. He was ready to get on the road.

Jack motioned to the kitchen counter. "Mind if I take a minute to make sure we know how you want things set up in your new apartment?"

"Sure," Nick answered.

He leaned on the other side of the counter, and looked down at the clipboard Jack had placed there. It held a stack of papers, and on top was a layout of the floor plan for his apartment in Baltimore.

"Wow. Didn't think about that part of it."

"That's not your job. But I've learned it is very helpful to get a clear idea of where our clients want us to put things. Cuts down on us making assumptions and then moving them a second time" Jack said.

"Guess that happens a lot if you don't ask, huh?" Nick replied. He noticed a few small beads of sweat on Jack's bald head.

"It used to. But I've learned that dollars are in the details, so I reached out to the Munsey and printed off this floor plan to be sure we got it right for you"

Nick chuckled. "I like that. Dollars are in the details. Used to be the devil, right?"

"Used to be. But in business, we've got to focus on the dollars," Jack explained. "Assumptions can be expensive."

Nick nodded with understanding.

They spent the next ten minutes talking and drawing onto the floor plan where Nick wanted the furniture and boxes arranged when they got it to his apartment building in Baltimore.

Nick was impressed with Jack's thoroughness and thoughtful questions.

After he was confident that he knew where Nick wanted his stuff, Jack reached out his hand.

"Thanks again for your business, Mister Turner! We'll be on our way in a few minutes and I appreciate you trusting us with your belongings."

Nick shook his hand.

Then, before he turned to leave, Jack hesitated.

"What is it?" Nick asked.

"Oh, I uh..." Jack paused.

He reached to grab his clipboard from the counter, then tapped it twice with his index finger.

"You weren't real clear earlier," he said, slowly.

Nick was a bit unsure where this was going, and his eyes squinted a bit but he remained quiet.

"I'm sorry. What I mean is," Nick explained, "when you asked us about the best teammate we've ever had…"

Nick's eyebrows lifted.

"See," Jack continued, "you got Rich's answer, but you didn't get mine. And this paper just reminded me of it."

"Oh, sorry. Guess I should have been more clear," Nick said. "So... who was it?"

Jack smiled with his whole face.

"Well, first, Rich really is a great teammate – but the best teammate I ever had is my wife."

Nick watched Jack's eyes brighten as he spoke of her.

"Not just because she's my wife though," Jack clarified. "I mean, she has been terrific about supporting me and going into business."

He grabbed the clipboard and pointed to it.

"But because of stuff like this. She's been my best teammate because she kept us in business."

Nick was curious. "Really?"

"Definitely. It may seem like it, but I am not really a detail guy. And early on, that cost us. Without her, we would have messed up half the jobs we've had – and probably gone bankrupt."

"So what did she do?" Nick asked.

"She is the one who told me something that changed how we did business. Before her, we were just another pair of guys with a truck. But she helped us go from no ratings to almost all five stars online. Isn't that how you found us?"

"It is." Nick confirmed.

"She saw me struggling and knew I was stressed a couple of months in. And she asked if she could help." Jack shook his head, reliving the experience. "I was afraid to show her the accounts and the stuff. I was afraid we were going to have to go back and ask for our old jobs. And she looked at them. And then she said something amazing."

He paused as he seemed to remember that moment.

"So… what'd she say?" Nick wanted to know.

"She said that 'all failure is the result of vagueness'"

Jack exhaled and explained further.

"Vague expectations. Vague directions. Vague answers. Vague questions. When we had done a poor job as movers, it was because we were too vague with all of that. And stuff like this," as he tapped the floor plan again, "is what made us better."

"Can you give me another example?" Nick asked.

"Sure. Think back to when you called us the first time. See, my wife is probably the one who answered. She's great about asking specific questions that help us identify what we can do the move for. That keeps our customers happy and still keeps our profit margins healthy."

"She did ask a lot of questions," Nick recalled.

"But did it feel annoying?"

"Not at all." Nick thought back to the first call. "In fact, it actually made me feel more important. I felt like she wanted to know so that your company could do a better job for me. She would say stuff like, 'just to be sure I write this down correctly, what I heard you say was…'"

Nick recalled her clarifying his every statement. "It was different… but it was nice. That's probably why I went with you guys."

Jack nodded and smiled with pride. "Yep. We hear that all the time now. But I didn't hear anything like it when I got started. We showed up and did what I assumed would be good enough. And often times it wasn't."

"Until your wife became your best teammate?"

"Truth is, it isn't just true for our business. Her help with us clarifying and asking questions to make sure we know what people need makes you better at everything. Especially being a husband."

"Really?"

"Definitely. I used to be just as bad in our relationship as I was with my moving clients. And I would blame my clients, or my wife, or other people for things that I should have done a better job of asking about. When you learn to ask questions and to give and request clear expectations, people appreciate you more. They trust you more..."

"And dollars are in the details!" Nick interrupted.

"You got it. And it is something that I am still working on, because Rich and I still make mistakes when we are working together. But I am much better than I used to be." Jack said.

There was an awkward pause while Nick considered that phrase again.

Almost on cue, Rich peeked into the empty apartment. "Alright, Jack. Your loyal crew just did an amazing job of loading everything else onto the truck!"

"Good timing," Jack answered. "Nick, thanks for letting me share a bit more than you probably expected."

Nick shook his head. "No... I really appreciate it. That was helpful."

"Alright, then." Jack walked toward Rich, who was still at the door. "We'll get everything in the new place just how you want it, Mister Turner. See you in Baltimore."

The two movers walked down the steps and toward their truck, then left.

Nick surveyed his empty apartment. It looked different.

Then Nick thought about what Jack had shared. That was true for more than just movers, wasn't it?

At the job he had just left, he could already think of half a dozen instances where his vagueness had led to expensive or time-consuming issues.

He had always blamed them on his boss or other workers. But maybe if he had asked more questions... if he had made sure to be more clear about what he saw and what he needed... maybe things would have been different.

Nick made his way through the apartment, checking one last time to be sure that nothing was left behind or forgotten in a drawer or closet.

When he had confirmed everything was packed away, he closed the door and locked it.

Then he took the door key off of his key ring and went outside to get into his Explorer.

He would drop the key off at the office and hit the road.

But when Nick got into the Explorer, he noticed the cardboard box he had left sitting on his passenger seat.

Inside was the scroll he had found earlier that morning, with the list of commandments for winning teammates.

He wondered if it could be true...

Then, after unrolling it to read the list, he couldn't believe his eyes.

Number two on the list was to Always Give and Request Clear Expectations.

That was just weird!

No… it was more than weird. Now he had to call his coach.

He took out his phone, found the number in his call log, and pressed the screen with his thumb.

A few second later, Coach Watkins voice was in his ear again.

"Well, this is twice in one day! Everything okay, Nicky?"

"Yes, sir. I'm just looking at the list you gave us back in high school, and you won't believe what's happened."

Coach Watkins breathed a bit louder, to let him know he was listening.

"So I asked the question you gave me, you know —about who is the best teammate you ever had?"

Just breathing again.

"And the guys I asked. Well, they gave interesting answers. And both of them made me think. But they were the first two answers on your list!"

"That is interesting!" Coach Watkins finally replied.

Nick stammered as he continued. "Yeah… the first guy talked about, uh, Remembering to Have Fun and Stay Positive… and, uh, the second guy talked about Always Giving and Requesting Clear Expectations! It was just so weird, you know?"

"Well, I'm glad you asked the question. Are you?"

"Am I what?" Nick asked, confused.

"Glad you asked."

"Oh, yeah. I guess so. I mean, both of them talked about it in terms of their jobs, but I thought about how it was true for our team, too," Nick said.

"That's important, Nicky," Coach said.

"Yes sir. Especially the second one. I mean, I know I wasn't always the most positive guy… but the one about expectations and asking questions and stuff hit me between the eyes."

Nick waited on Coach Watkins to ask, but just heard the same patient breathing.

"You remember that game against Franklin my senior year, when I got so mad at you for taking me right back out?"

"I do."

"Well, I didn't understand how important it was to give and get clear expectations. I didn't ask who I was going in for. I didn't ask what defense we were going to be in or who I was guarding. I deserved to come right back out. That's why you took me out, right?" Nick asked.

"You didn't want me to make a mistake."

"That's part of it," Coach said.

"What do you mean, part of it?"

"Well, other mistakes would have followed, but the one you came out for was not caring enough to ask and clarify things that should have been more important to you. When you assumed and didn't ask, you told your team that you weren't focused enough on your team's success. And that is a dangerous message to send."

Nick understood even better now.

"So you let people know how much you care by how much you are willing to ask? By how committed you are to do things right?" Nick asked.

"You're a smart kid, Nicky. Glad you called."

"Thanks, Coach. I may be calling you again before too long. Still have almost a day's worth of asking that question left," Nick joked.

"Glad to hear it, Nicky. Travel safe."

"Okay. Bye, Coach." Nick hung up and placed the phone in the console. He turned the key and appreciated hearing the roar of the engine as it came to life.

He had a long way to go.

CHAPTER 4

frequently share appreciation and thanks

Nick was not happy about leaving Atlanta, but he was excited about the possibility of a fresh start and career opportunity in Baltimore.

He had looked over the driving directions a handful of times, and knew that he'd be traveling 85 north almost all the way to Raleigh, NC. Because the trip was over ten hours long, he had reserved a hotel room outside Raleigh, and he would finish the trip the next day.

The trip would carry him very close to his sister's house in Chapel Hill, but he didn't want to get into that. He was busy moving.

His sister and her stuff could wait a few days, he decided.

Most of the next few hours consisted of

him singing out loud to himself, letting his phone shuffle play songs and then laughing at himself when he would get caught by other drivers playing his own personal game of vehicular karaoke.

By mid-afternoon, Nick was getting hungry, and began looking for an exit with ample restaurant options.

He didn't want fast food, so when he pulled off the highway somewhere just north of Greenville he was pleased to see a clean looking diner in a shopping center just a couple of streets off the exit.

He stretched his legs a bit after parking, felt the heat of the afternoon sun, and went inside. The smell of fresh baked breads filled the air.

"Welcome to Stacks!" A woman's voice greeted him as the door closed behind him.

He looked up, and the lady was coming toward him, her smile and big teeth flanked on each side by crows' feet that marked her age.

She pointed to her chest where a name tag told him the same thing her southern drawl did. "Mornin'! My name's Gwen."

Nick gave a faint smile as reply.

"Your first time here? Well, don't you worry none. Gwen'll take good care of you!"

She led him to a booth and placed a menu on the table.

Another waitress, this one much younger, delivered his utensils. They were wrapped neatly inside a cloth napkin.

"Why thank you, Julie! You are so sweet!" Gwen said.

Then she turned back to Nick. "She is so helpful. Now you take a look at that and let me know if anything looks good enough to order."

Gwen's champagne colored hair fell around her shoulders in long bleached curls, contrasting sharply with the black shirts that she, and all employees, were wearing. It appeared almost transparent when it caught the sunshine from the window.

"I can get you something to drink if you like?" She said.

"Just water right now," Nick requested.

Gwen smiled. "Coming up," she said, and she made her way back over to the counter, where she grabbed three plates that were going to another table.

He saw her nod and say something to the cook. An instant later, the cook stood up a bit straighter and smiled to himself as she walked away with the food.

Nick opened up and looked over the menu, and when he looked back up there was a glass of water in front of him. Gwen was on the other side of the restaurant talking with a dark haired waitress.

She sure does seem happy, he thought. A lot happier than he would expect an over-50 waitress to be...

He watched her for a minute or two, and was impressed at the impact she had on her coworkers. Each time she left one of them, they seemed to be more positive.

Even the people at her tables were affected. When she left the bill at one table, Nick noticed the two men both beaming at her when she spoke to them.

It was almost three o'clock in the afternoon, and Gwen was a fountain of energy.

When she returned to take his order, he began to get an idea why.

"Alrighty, so here I am again. Now who do I have the pleasure of serving today?"

"I'm Nick."

"Thank you, Nick. I am so glad you are here! Now were you able to decide on anything yet or could I help you with a suggestion?"

"I was thinking about the Philly cheesesteak. With sweet potato fries?"

"Excellent choice! I'll get that in for you right now. Anything else?" She asked.

"No, ma'am." Nick answered.

He would ask her when she came back with his food. She was busy now, and he watched her refilling another table's drinks.

He turned his attention back to his trip. He'd be in Raleigh tonight and then would make it to Baltimore by dinnertime tomorrow. And if Jack and Rich took care of things like they had discussed, his apartment furniture would be waiting there for him, along with the boxes he would need to unpack.

He thought about the list of ten commandments for winning teammates.

The paper was still in his Explorer, laying in the box where he had put it.

It had been a funny coincidence that he had found them, but he wasn't sure how much that list would really help him with his next job. Doing IT project work was much more about knowledge and skills than that touchy-feely stuff…

He took a drink of his water, and as he went to put it back down the dark haired waitress was there with a pitcher to refill it.

"Wow, you're quick!" he said.

"Well, I like to help Gwen out. She is great to work with."

"Aw, honey, thank you!" Gwen's voice arrived before she did. "You are so thoughtful! I appreciate you taking such good care of my table."

The dark haired waitress blushed and

moved on to refill other tables as well.

"She's a pretty good teammate, huh?" He said.

Gwen looked over at her. "Oh, yes. She's a sweetheart."

"Gwen, do you have time for me to ask you a question?" Nick asked.

"Why sure, honey. What is it?"

Nick hesitated again. "Okay, well, it's probably gonna sound a little weird."

"Honey, weird is wonderful!" She looked at him warmly. "So, what's your question?"

"Okay," Nick began. "I'd like to know who is the best teammate you ever had."

Gwen smiled, then her lips went flat in thoughtfulness, and then she spoke.

"Tell you what. I'm supposed to get off at three − been working since morning shift. I'll come back and tell you after I clock out, okay?"

Nick nodded, and she left his table. He saw her go to the back.

A few minutes later, she returned. In her left hand she was carrying his lunch plate, and in her right was his ticket.

"You're my last table of the day. Would it be too awkward if I sat down to answer your question while you ate?"

"Not at all," Nick replied.

Gwen sat across from him and waited a

moment before she began.

Nick ate a couple of the warm sweet potato fries as she started.

"That question you asked made me think a bit," Gwen said. "I'm guessing that's why you asked it… because a good question makes you think a while about it. So I appreciate you asking it, and I think I know what my answer is."

Gwen smiled, and Nick again noticed the wrinkles around her eyes. But this time they seemed deeper, earned by experiences.

Nick stopped eating and listened.

"The question was tough for me," she said, "because I've been alone through most of my life. I had a good childhood and good parents, but I moved to Florida after I graduated from school and I've been on my own since then."

Nick sat motionless as she continued her story.

"I was married to a Navy pilot for nine years and we had a boy, but he was never there as a father or as my teammate. And when he came home after he was in a jet crash he kind of went off the deep end." She paused and took a breath.

"Even before the violence started, I had been on my own. But after the divorce I took our son and left town. There were churches and neighbors who helped, but nobody that was really there as a teammate. So I thought about it, and there was only one person who was there when my parents passed and supporting me when I wanted to do whatever crazy thing I had in my mind to do. That was my sister."

She took another breath, and Nick could see that she was remembering someone she cared deeply about.

"Sounds like a special lady," he said.

"She was. She loved me and encouraged me and always took the time to tell me how much I meant to her."

Nick saw her squint her eyes, and she rubbed one with her finger.

"Somebody who makes you feel appreciated and important. That's the best teammate you can have, I think. And I'm telling you because I hate that I didn't tell her that."

Nick swallowed the air in his mouth and felt her emotion.

Gwen smiled at him again. "You know what she used to ask me?"

"What's that?" he asked.

"She'd say to me 'if everything you took for granted was taken away, what would you be left with?' I didn't get it back then. Then when I lost her to a car accident, it finally made sense to me. So I work hard to be grateful for my son… for everybody I meet and everybody I work with, 'cause that's important. And maybe I overdo it, but I don't think people mind."

She laughed, coming back from her story into reality.

"'Course, I suppose you didn't expect to get that much of an answer, did you honey?'"

Nick laughed with her, and they both felt more comfortable.

"You know, Gwen," he said, grabbing a few more fries, "I couldn't imagine a more terrific answer. Thank you for sharing it with me"

She nodded.

"Okay, honey. You finish that meal and have a great rest of your day. I'll grab that check whenever you're ready. And thanks for asking me your question!"

Nick nodded as Gwen got up from the table.

The sandwich was excellent, but he barely tasted it as he chewed. He ate slowly, thinking about her sister.

When he was finished, he took out enough cash for the meal and a generous tip and placed it with the check. He had not seen Gwen since she had left his table, and he thought that maybe she had left.

But as he took a last sip of water from his glass, she was back at his table, wearing the same smile that she had greeted him when he first arrived.

"Hi Nick. Can I get you a to-go cup?"

"No, ma'am. I need to get back on the road. But I truly appreciate your story. I seem to be learning a lot today, and it turns out that seeing you and hearing your story was another important lesson for me. Can I ask you another question?"

"Sure, honey." She nodded and began to clean up his table.

"Why do your thank you's seem more powerful than the ones I seem to give?"

"It's not just the thank you, it's the thing you are thankful for. You have to be specific about what you appreciate. Most people just say thanks, but it's a vague and absentminded expression. A real thank you includes a 'for.' I never just say thanks, honey. I say, 'thank you for caring enough to refill those glasses. You saved me from another nickel tip and I can't wait to return the favor!'"

Gwen paused to let that sink in. "You got to be sure they know why you are thankful and how it made you feel. That's the secret to making people really feel appreciated."

"I never thought about that," Nick admitted.

"Seems like we're all here learning something. You know the main thing I learned from my sister?"

"No, what is it?"

"Honey, she taught me that people love to feel appreciated. But that wasn't the most important thing. See, when you frequently share appreciation and thanks, you have a better day, too."

She winked at him, as if sharing a secret. "Turns out that gratefulness is the door to happiness. That's what my sister knew long before I did. She was always being thankful… and I suppose I was just a slow learner."

She had collected his plate and was ready to carry it away.

Nick stood up. "It was a real pleasure to meet you, Gwen. You have a great day."

"I will. And thank you for coming in. Your question made my day"

She smiled one last time and turned away, and he made his way back to the Explorer.

The first thing he did after starting the engine was call Coach Watkins again.

"Yeah?"

"Coach – hey, it's Nick again."

"Yeah. How's the trip, Nicky?"

"Turns out it's going really well, actually," Nick said. "I just wanted to say thank you. I guess I never did that until now. But you did your best to teach us a bunch of stuff, and I just wasn't yet ready to hear it back then."

Coach Watkins breathed a moment, then said "That means a lot, Nicky. Thank you."

"Coach, you used to say something to us about, uh, what gets praised?"

"What gets rewarded gets repeated?" Watkins asked.

"Yes, sir. That's the one! You meant we should let people on the team know when they did something well so they would do it again."

"That's true, Nicky. In fact," he continued, "I read somewhere the other day that in Sweden they send out a text message to people who donate blood to thank them when their blood saves someone's life. Everybody wants to feel good about themselves. And all it takes is a little mindfulness and a few kind words."

Nick looked down at the rolled paper still laying near the top of the cardboard box beside him. Halfway to himself, Nick said "and those words lift both people."

"Yep. And as a coach, that was a lesson I didn't learn as soon as I should have. When I started, I thought my job was to see the gap between where somebody was and where they needed to be... then to get them to close that gap. Offensive skills, defensive effort, talking, grades... I saw the gap, and I worked hard at driving people to close it. But that didn't always work out so well..."

"Why not?" Nick asked. He felt the air conditioning beginning to cool the interior.

"Well, Nicky, because people don't like to always be told what's wrong. They need to know that you also see a lot of what they're doing right."

Coach Watkins paused and breathed a moment.

Nick tried to summarize the idea. "You had to learn to appreciate the doughnut, and not just complain about the hole."

"Exactly. And some coaches and coworkers never learn how important it is to see and actually say something about those good things."

"I'm glad you gave me that question, Coach," Nick said, sincerely.

"Good... But you're not gonna call me every few hours, are you?" Watkins asked.

"Ha... No, sir." Nick answered, laughing. "But I can't promise anything about tomorrow."

"Well, I'll look forward to hearing more then, Nicky. Travel safe."

"Yes sir." And Nick hung up. But before he put the phone down to drive off, he wanted to send a text.

"Hey Abs. Just wanted to say thanks for being a good sister. I'll call tomorrow."

And a few minutes later he was back on 85 north.

CHAPTER 5

continue to grow and stay coachable

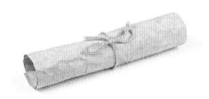

It was after seven o'clock when his Explorer came to a stop in the parking lot of the Durham Hampton Inn.

Nick had prepared a small backpack with clothes and stuff for tonight, and he reached into the back seat to grab it. The sun was beginning to set behind a collection of pine trees as he walked toward the sliding glass doors to check in.

He checked his phone again, but there was no reply from his sister yet.

Nick didn't see anyone else when he got inside the hotel, then he was surprised when he saw the person behind the desk.

It was a tall, older gentleman with head full

of neatly combed white hair. He wore a pale blue oxford shirt with dark pants and looked at Nick over the top of his reading glasses, which he carefully put down next to the large book he had been reading.

"Good evening, Sir! Welcome to the Hampton Inn. Do you have a reservation?"

"Yes," Nick said, setting his backpack on the floor. "Nick Turner. One night."

The older man smiled, searched his computer screen, and looked back up at Nick.

"We have you in room 319, Mister Turner."

"So what are you reading?" Nick asked, making small talk. It had been a long ride, and it was nice to hear another voice.

The older man flipped the book over and read the cover. "Contemporary Sociological Theory," he chuckled. "Not a best seller, but it is interesting."

Nick was surprised.

"Don't see a lot of hotel workers reading that, I guess," Nick replied.

"No, sir. Probably not. But I've been told I'm a bit of a weird bird." The older man reached over the counter and extended two room cards toward Nick.

"Thank you, uh…"

"Arthur" the older man said. "You can call me Arthur. And your room is on our third floor.

Breakfast at six am right over there."

He pointed to the buffet tables and eating area.

Nick began to walk away with his keys and backpack, but with the hotel lobby empty except for him and the desk clerk, he thought it was a perfect opportunity to ask.

"Excuse me, Arthur."

"Yes sir?"

"Before you go back to your intimidating book, I wondered if I could ask you a question," Nick said.

"Oh, I love a good question," Arthur said. "Shoot!"

"Okay, it's a little weird. I promised a friend that I would ask everyone I met, though, so here it is… Who is the best teammate you ever had?"

Arthur grabbed his reading glasses and chewed on one of the ear pieces as he thought about what Nick had asked him. "Oh, now that's a good one, isn't it?" he said to himself.

Nick looked outside to see if anyone else was coming in, but the lobby and front entrance area were still theirs alone.

"Okay, I know who it would be," Arthur put on his glasses and placed his hands on his hips as he gave his answer.

"It was a guy named Will. Will Thomas. We grew up in the same town, worked together one summer when I was in school, and he was the best teammate I ever had."

"Why was that?" Nick prompted.

Arthur leaned over with his forearm on the counter as he spoke. "I didn't have any brothers or sisters, and didn't see much of my dad, because he liked drinking more than working. So I just about lived with Will. And his dad was one of the football coaches at the high school."

Arthur peeked outside at the parking lot to see if there would be any interruption to his story, and seeing no customers there he continued.

"Now we were both at practice every day, but I never played much in games. I was always much better with numbers than I was with helmets... and I guess it probably bothered Will's dad that he wasn't a better athlete than he was... but Will was a worker. And it was out there on the freshly cut grass that he taught me what it meant to work hard and scratch and claw for something you want. My parents never did that."

He stopped the story to think about something, then his eyes returned to Nick a moment later.

"I was taller and stronger than he was, but Will was a better player. Watching Will is what gave me my work ethic. And even though it didn't help me with football, I am here today because of what I used to hear his dad saying to him."

Nick was mesmerized. It amazed him how much people were willing to share if you just moved beyond small talk and asked something meaningful.

"What did he say to his son?" Nick requested.

"He told him that if he wanted to be good at anything, he had to be coachable."

Nick's face wrinkled a bit. "That's it?" he asked.

"Oh, no. There was much more to it. He liked to say that uncoachable kids turn into unmanageable adults. He had just seen so many players not get better because they thought they knew it all or thought they were good enough. And he said that most people stop improving because they are more interested in validation than in being coachable. And I'll tell you what… he was right."

"So did he go into any detail?" Nick asked.

"Oh, yes. Here… I'll show you." And Arthur grabbed a piece of paper from the printer beside his computer to draw on. "I bet it's been twenty years since I drew this!"

Nick watched Arthur's pen draw a circle, and then watched as he wrote a capitol letter H on the top, bottom and on both sides.

"Okay, I give up," Nick said. "What are those H's for?"

"Honest, Hungry, Humble, and Habits." Arthur slid the paper across the counter to Nick, but it was still nothing more than a circle and four H's.

"Go ahead and write them down so you remember," Arthur suggested, offering the pen.

Nick took the pen.

"Will was a great teammate because he was coachable. That's what made him so good. Not just at football, but later on in business, too."

Nick wondered to himself… if this was such great information, why was Arthur working behind the desk of a hotel at his age?

But he wrote the word honest and listened intently as Arthur continued.

"Will's dad told him, told us, that the first thing you have to do is be honest about where you are. To admit your circumstances and behavior. To know what you are. And a lot of people don't want to do that. They want to see the airbrushed version of themselves in the mirror instead of the real truth." Arthur nodded as he said this, for emphasis.

"Bet you probably know somebody like that, don't you?" Arthur asked.

Nick smiled in agreement, but let him keep talking.

"Then the second H is for hungry. You have to want something that you don't have. You have to have something you want to be or to accomplish. Will's dad said sometimes it was his job to describe the thing that they couldn't see well enough that they were hungry for it. But to be coachable, he said you had to want something."

He waited to see Nick write the word hungry.

"All right. After that, the third H is for Humble. Will's dad said that you had to be humble enough to take advice from more knowledgeable people." He laughed to himself and then explained. "Will sometimes got frustrated listening to his dad's sayings, and he'd repeat them with this funny voice. He'd drop his voice as deep as he could and say, 'confidence is thinking you can help, ego is thinking you don't need help'"

Nick laughed out loud, hearing Arthur try to mimic his friends comical voice.

"Oh yeah. But mostly he was a good teammate because of the last H. Will showed me how important it was to choose good habits. He was a great kid. Did his homework every night. Made his bed in the morning. He would shrug it off back then, and tell me that doing the right thing is just as easy as doing the wrong thing, so might as well do it right all the time. I remember that…"

Arthur paused when he heard the glass doors of the lobby slide open. Two nicely dressed women walked in together with rolling luggage.

Nick wrote Habits on the paper, held it up to show Arthur, and put the pen on the counter.

"I'll be back down later, Arthur, Okay?"

"Yes, sir, Mr. Turner," he waved. And then he warmly greeted the two ladies.

Nick went upstairs to find his room, then unpacked his backpack and showered.

By the time he looked at the clock again, it was nearly 9:30 at night.

And he had reached the third H.

He was hungry.

He got dressed in nice shorts and a collared knit shirt and made his way back to the front desk. He was pleased to see Arthur was still there, and alone again.

"Okay, Arthur. I've got to eat something. Any place you'd recommend that would sell me an adult beverage or two?"

"Yes, sir. You'll like Tobacco Road. I can draw you directions!"

"And was there anything else you wanted to share about Will being the best teammate you ever had?" Nick asked.

"Oh… well, I suppose I could put a bow on it. We were talking about habits, right?"

"Yes, sir," Nick confirmed.

"Well, Will's dad used to tell us that knowing and doing were two awfully different things. He'd say, 'Will, now most everybody knows what to do, but the successful ones make a habit of doing it.'"

Arthur used the same deep voice from earlier for Will's dad.

"And he'd tell Will and me that making a mistake is an education, but repeating a mistake was foolishness. He'd say that you choose your habits just like you choose your friends… and if you choose good ones, they will take care of you."

Arthur took a deep breath and then exhaled slowly. "I didn't know it then, but I like to think that he was talking about me. He was a good man. And Will helped me to grow and stay honest and hungry. He was a great teammate."

"Sounds like it," Nick agreed. "And so now you are reading books like that…" Nick pointed to the thick book on the counter – "to keep learning?"

Arthur looked down at the thick book he had been reading when time permitted.

"That's right. This sociology stuff is actually interesting. I learned about business my first time through. Like I said, I was always good with numbers. So I figured I would try to learn more about people this time. I'm working on a degree at the university. And the older you get, the more you realize that business is knowing people."

Nick was impressed with him. And after hearing him speak, Nick was surprised that a man with that kind of drive was working behind a hotel desk.

Arthur finished drawing the map he had promised.

"Okay, then… Guess I'll give it a try." Nick took the restaurant directions that Arthur had written down for him and walked out through the glass doors.

Chapter 6

be aware of and encourage others

Instead of sitting alone at a table, Nick made his way to the bar.

Tobacco Road was an upscale sports bar that had flat screen TVs everywhere. It was more than half full after nine o'clock on a weeknight, and the hum of conversations that surrounded him as he entered gave it a nice energy.

There were two bartenders keeping up with demand for drinks, both of them guys about Nick's age. The one with a beard walked over to greet him.

"Welcome to Tobacco Road! My name is Tom. What can I get you?"

"Guinness, please!" Nick took out his

license, as he still got carded regularly.

"Thanks..." Tom checked his ID, then returned it. "Get you a menu?"

"That'd be great," Nick said.

The bar was dark brown and clean, and Nick chose a stool away from the other bar patrons. Behind the bar were shelves of brightly lit liquor bottles and a wall of draft beer taps to choose from. Above the beer taps were a row of more flat screens with various games being broadcast.

Tom provided the menu, and returned to check on another guy further down the bar.

Nick took Tom's advice and ordered a buffalo chicken sandwich. He was halfway through the meal before he noticed how Tom and his coworkers were interacting.

They were persistently talking to each other when they weren't helping customers.

It was a busy night, but the wait staff and bar staff talked constantly. They all appeared to be short comments... but Nick was curious to know what they were saying.

He watched Tom saying goodbye to a couple that had eaten at the bar, giving them a thumbs up as they left. Tom spent a moment with the other guy a few seats down the bar, then made his way over to check on Nick.

"Sandwich good?" He asked.

"Yeah. It is," Nick responded.

"So what are you in town for?" Tom wiped his hands on a towel.

Nick finished the bite he had just taken before answering. "Traveling to Baltimore. Got a new job there..."

"Nice!" Tom said. "What kind of work you do?"

Nick drank the last of his beverage. "I'm an IT project guy. Lot's of programming and development work."

"That's impressive. Bet you'll do a great job there," Tom said.

"Thanks. Hope so..." Nick held up his glass to request a refill as Tom started to walk away. "Hey, can I ask you a question?"

"Sure. Let me grab you another one!"

Tom was back a minute later handing Nick a full glass. "So, what's your question?"

"I noticed you and your coworkers are always talking to each other. Not just a little, though – I mean, it's like every moment you're not with a customer you are finding somebody to say something to."

"Yeah... we do!"

"So I was just wondering," Nick said. "What are you saying to them?"

Tom smiled. "It's part of the job here. Kind of a daily competition to see who can do it the most. No prize or anything, but it's fun…"

He realized that Nick didn't understand what he had said.

"Reminders and Encouragements. It's the most important part of our job. That's what we are saying to each other. Just reminders…"

"Like what?" Nick asked.

"Like 'don't forget to refill the napkins,' or 'remember to bus your area.' There's a thousand things we could say… but we have fun with it. And as silly as it sounds, it helps us do a better job."

"And it's part of your training?"

"Not when I first got here. But after Julia came, it just caught on. We made fun of her at first, but then we saw how much smoother things were when we talked all the time."

Nick took a drink, then nodded. "And so where is Julia now?"

"You actually just missed her. She's in charge of staff training for all of our restaurants now. So she still stops by a lot."

"And that's all she did? Just reminded people around her what they needed to do? Wouldn't that get annoying?"

"Not the way she did it," Tom said. He left to pour a few drinks and check on the other guy, who was nibbling on the remaining portion of his huge plate of nachos.

When he retuned to Nick, he picked up where he had left off.

"But when she explained it, she said the most important thing was to get people feeling better about what's ahead of them in the windshield, not to focus what's behind them in the rearview mirror. She said most people get caught up making rearview criticisms – but you can't change what's already happened. So our job is to help the people around us think about what needs to happen next for things to go well."

"So what is a rearview criticism?"

"Just looking back and complaining about something. People used to get upset and ask 'why didn't you get the food out faster.' But that just upset people and didn't solve anything. Instead, when you give reminders to get the food out, you can make sure that people all have a better experience. Stuff gets done."

"And it doesn't feel like nagging?" Nick asked.

"Not if you say it the right way. You're in IT, right? Computers and stuff?"

Nick nodded.

"So are there details that you and your teammates sometimes didn't pay attention to? Things that if you shared a few reminders you could keep those mistakes from happening?"

"Okay, I see what you mean..." Nick said.

There were dozens of things he could have said at his last two jobs that he hadn't.

Tom continued and brought Nick back from his memories of his last jobs. "And you have to know the person you are working with. That's another thing Julia emphasized. Like I said… we have fun with it. It's almost a game now to see who can see what needs to be done. It creates more awareness."

Nick thought that made sense. But before he went any further, he realized that he still hadn't asked the question that would keep his promise to Coach Watkins.

"Okay. So I have another question for you," Nick announced.

Tom nodded. "No problem. Let me catch up and I'll be back asap."

Nick watched the soccer game that was on. He had never played soccer, but as he watched he noticed that even they were talking to each other on the field.

He thought back to his high school basketball team.

They hadn't shared very many reminders or encouragements. He knew for sure that he hadn't. He had actually probably been the guy who barked out some of those rearview criticisms Tom described.

Had he been like that at his last job, too?

Tom slapped the bar when he came back. "Okay, I'm yours."

"So, it's a little weird. But I'd like to know who you would say is the best teammate that you ever had?"

Nick watched his face shift as he thought through a few different ideas.

"Huh… Never thought about that. I mean I played sports all through school, right? But the more I think about it, it wasn't anybody from football or lacrosse. A couple of good choices, but not the best. I'd have to say that the best teammate I ever had was the woman I've already told you about. Julia."

"Why Julia, then?" Nick probed.

"Julia started here as a waitress. And I told you about the whole reminders and encouragements thing. But she was somebody that just cared about people. She made you feel like you mattered."

"How'd she do that?"

Tom rubbed his chin. "She used to say that you have to know three things about the people you spend time with – their passions, their problems, and their personality… She'd ask questions to get to know you, just like you were her family. And the better she knew you, the more you talked to her, the more comfortable you were sharing those reminders and encouraging people. Even about stuff outside of work."

"Anything else you can share about her?" Nick asked.

He was just about finished with his second Guinness and Tom had already cleared away his empty plate.

"Nah… but I know she's the reason it's so great to work here now. When I got here, things were fine. But with her, things are just better. People look to notice stuff about your job… but even more, they notice stuff about you. I think it's mostly that she taught us to be more aware of the needs that are around us."

"Like refills?" Nick kidded.

"Yeah, that. But other stuff, too. Like when you are having a bad day, people notice and they encourage you. See that guy?"

Tom pointed at one of the waiters.

"He's struggling with year one of law school. And in the middle of my reminders about his drink orders, I make sure to mention his law degree. But I wouldn't have known or even cared if Julia hadn't started asking about and encouraging the rest of us."

"I don't know, man." Nick said.

"What?"

"You think everybody needs encouragement?" he asked, disbelieving.

"Well, there is a test." Tom smiled, sure of himself. "The surest way to know if somebody needs encouragement is with a breath test... if you see that they're breathing, they need encouragement!"

Nick laughed and paid his tab, leaving a healthy tip for his new favorite bartender.

Tom went back to busying himself behind the bar, sharing comments with his coworkers again, and Nick got up to leave.

"Good luck in Baltimore, man!" Tom called.

Nick waved his hand, then was on his way back to the hotel for some rest.

He still had six hours of driving ahead of him in the morning.

CHAPTER 7

do more than is expected with enthusiasm

It was after eleven when Nick walked back through the glass doors into the hotel lobby.

The front desk was occupied by a young black woman. She had on a white collared shirt and a name tag.

"Arthur gone?"

"Yes, sir," she said. "Can I help you with something?"

As he got closer, he saw her name was Kayla. He shook his head and began to walk toward the elevators, ready to get some sleep.

But before he got too far from the front desk, he stopped. He was curious.

"So you just relieved him... You're the graveyard shift?" he asked.

"I suppose. Here from eleven 'til seven."

"Do you know long Arthur's been working here? He seemed like a really good guy."

She smiled. "Since before we opened, I guess. I've only been here about six months, but he's a terrific guy to work for."

She spoke of him with a very respectful tone.

Nick didn't quite understand. "Work FOR?" He asked. "What do you mean?"

Kayla twisted her neck a bit to show her surprise. "Mr. Duncan doesn't work here. He just likes filling in sometimes. He was here helping out our regular afternoon guy."

She pointed to a frame on the wall to her left. It was a certificate.

Above a picture of the hotel, in dark blue letters that matched the logo, it said, "This franchise location proudly owned and operated by Arthur Duncan."

No way. He was the owner?

Nick stared at the words for a few seconds, then collected himself.

"Okay. Wow... I didn't know that."

"You wouldn't, just talking to him..." she said.

He peeked behind the counter. "You keep a book back there, like he does?"

Before she answered, he noticed her eyes

focusing on something on the other side of the lobby. "Excuse me just a moment," she said.

Kayla walked past him into the sitting area of the lobby where, behind the legs of one of the tables, she had seen a small piece of paper on the floor.

She picked it up, walked it over to a trash can, and returned to their conversation.

"Sorry. It's a habit. Can't stand to see stuff like that." She explained. Then she answered him. "But no books for me, while I'm here. I can usually find something to do to keep myself busy."

"I see that," Nick said. "Well, good night. See you for breakfast?"

"Yes, sir. At least until seven!"

And Nick went up to his room to try and rest...

The next morning, his phone alarm woke him at 5:45.

Nick got dressed quickly and left his backpack on the bed to go grab something to eat.

He wanted to get an early start on his drive to Baltimore, and was excited to see his stuff in the new apartment. His new job started tomorrow!

By 6:15, the breakfast buffet area was already bustling with about a dozen other people grabbing fruit, yogurt, oatmeal, and cereal.

Nick fixed a cup of coffee and looked over behind the front desk, where Kayla and a heavyset man were standing together in conversation with a guest.

The man beside Kayla had on a white oxford shirt and a similar looking name tag.

The guest seemed to be upset about something, stabbing at his paperwork on the counter with his index finger - but even after nearly eight hours of being on duty Kayla maintained a warm smile.

With a few words she seemed to transform his anger into appreciation, and the heavyset guy was waving goodbye to the satisfied guest as Nick arrived.

"Everything okay?" He asked, inquisitively.

"Perfect!" Kayla replied. "Hope you had a nice stay with us."

"I did. Thank you. Gotta go grab my bag upstairs, but I wanted to ask you a question before I left. Do you have a minute?"

Kayla surveyed the crowd of eating guests for a moment, then looked briefly at the heavyset guy.

"Sure. Marcus can cover for a minute or three. Is it about Arthur?"

"Actually, no. I just promised a friend that I'd ask this question when I met people... It's a little strange, I know... but I'd like to hear your answer."

Kayla looked a bit uncertain, but curious. "Sure. So, what's your question?"

They walked over to stand near the collection of stylish blue and green upholstered chairs on the other side of the lobby.

"Okay. I just want to know... who is the best teammate you've ever had?"

Kayla paused, surprised by the question.

"Wasn't expecting that," she said.

"I know. But is there somebody that comes to your mind?" He questioned.

"Without a doubt..." She announced. "It's my momma."

"Okay... why her?"

"You really want to know?" she asked.

Nick's eyes widened with sincerity. "I do."

Kayla considered her response. "She always did more than just her job. She was all about finding ways to make things around her better... finding ways to help people. Momma loved it. And even though she had all kinds of reasons to be angry or complain about how unfair things were, I don't think I ever saw her go a day without smiling."

"Can you share an example for me?" he requested. "What she did, and why?"

She glanced over at Marcus to confirm that he had things at the desk under control.

"She told me a story once," Kayla shared.

"And I think it's why she ended up being the woman that she was."

Nick adjusted himself in the chair to listen a bit better.

"When I was young, momma worked at a big hotel in Charlotte as a housekeeper. She said that she was all about herself. Did her job and went home. Didn't want to bother or fool with anybody else and their problems. Then one day she almost lost her job..."

Kayla waited for Nick to grasp the consequences of that loss.

"She said that she should have been fired. Said we should have been on the street and hungry. Because she had lost her keys. See, back then, housekeepers didn't have those electronic cards. Her big nice hotel had keys."

She laughed, staring out vaguely as she recalled her mother's story.

"Well, momma – who had been just as unconcerned as she could be about her coworkers, who never took a moment to smile at or assist them – she realizes that she doesn't have her keys. And she goes looking for them and can't find them and finally she goes to the manager to admit what had happened. And she knew that it was likely the end of her working there."

"So what happened?" Nick asked, anxiously.

"Momma told me she went to see the manager, and that when she was getting off the service elevator one of those women who she had been ignoring the whole time she had worked there stopped her in the hallway. Said that she had started to cry... and then that nice woman who she had never cared a bit about grabbed her arm and smiled the kindest smile you ever saw and held up the keys to ask if they were hers. Said she had found them on the floor of the laundry room, and she didn't want my momma getting in any trouble for it."

Nick saw the gratefulness even now in Kayla's eyes for that random act of kindness.

"She was picking up things for somebody else that she didn't have to. And that changed my momma's life. And my momma spent the rest of her life picking things up for others, because she learned that people love you for it... and that you feel good after doing it."

"That's a great story," Nick commented.

"Not just a story to me. It's how I grew up. And it's how I live, now. See, as a manager, you want people who see themselves as a small part of something bigger than themselves. You want people who do more than they have to. You don't want compliance. Employees are compliant. Complainers are compliant. You want people who care about the people around them… who are willing to pick things up and watch out for each other."

"So how do you get them to do that?" Nick asked. "I mean, it sounds terrific, but not everybody has the same experience your mom did, right?"

"Right," She admitted. "That's where I come in. My job is to be the person I want my team to be."

He looked at her, puzzled.

"Enthusiasm is a choice people make. You choose to be positive and have energy. And as a leader, if I'm not enthusiastic about doing more than just my job, nobody else will be, either. Being enthusiastic and helping others isn't something you're born with, like height or eye color. It is a choice. Momma said that 'it may not always be easy, but it will always be worth it.' And now that I'm older, I know what she meant."

"So how do you keep yourself up all the time?" Nick asked.

"I look for ways to help. I train my eyes to see others and their needs, not just my own. Because momma was right… you feel better when you are helpful. You don't have to volunteer to do more, but you always turn out a better person when you do. It's the unassigned work you do that sets you apart, right? So, I try to always ask myself the question, 'if everyone did and cared as much as me, what kind of company would we be?'"

She sounded like Coach Watkins used to. Nick began to understand that he hadn't been the best teammate back in school. He hadn't thought to pick up things for others, and he certainly had not been enthusiastic about it.

He hadn't picked things up for others at his last two jobs, either. He even remembered walking by and leaving trash laying on the ground, convinced that it was somebody else's job. Convinced that he didn't need to concern himself with that stuff.

And he remembered Coach Watkins talking about how the best players were the ones who did stuff that never showed up on a statistics report. The ones that saw when something needed to be done and did it without being asked.

Nick realized that managers and coaches were a lot alike.

"So to answer your question," Kayla interrupted his thoughts, "it's my mom, because she showed me that leadership is serving and inspiring others."

"Sounds like Arthur would have liked your mom too," Nick said.

"I think so," she agreed. "When I was still

in college, I got this job as manager because I did more than most people expected. He said it showed I was hungry, but I was just doing what my momma had taught me. I filled in more than the blanks. I asked questions about the team I would be working with, not just about my salary. I told him I thought a leader's job was to pick up things for others."

"Like that paper last night," Nick recalled.

"Sure. A lot like that." She agreed, and looking back at the front desk she saw that Marcus needed her.

"Hope that helps you. Enjoyed the chance to share it!" she said, and hurried over to the counter with a heartfelt smile.

Nick went to his room, grabbed his bag, and made his way back downstairs to leave.

This was turning into a pretty interesting trip.

With his backpack in hand, he grabbed a banana and a coffee refill from the buffet.

He waved his thanks to Kayla at around 6:55, and then was outside the glass doors and climbing into his Explorer for another long drive.

The cardboard box was there beside him on the passenger seat, and inside it was the scroll that had started all of this.

He unrolled it again to survey the list.

Remember to have fun, Give and request clear expectations. Share appreciation and thanks. Stay coachable. Be aware of and encourage others. Do more than is expected with enthusiasm…

Nick wanted to call coach again.

He would need to get gas and pick up lunch somewhere, and he hoped to make it to his new home before dinnertime.

CHAPTER 8

respect the clock and the calendar

Nick had driven nearly a hundred miles before he looked down and noticed an unread text message.

It was from his sister.

He could feel the warmth of the bright sunlight coming through the passenger window, and the glare made it difficult to read the screen on his phone.

When he held it in the shadows beneath the dash he was able to read it more clearly.

"Give me a call when you can," it said.

It was after nine am, and he was getting hungry. That coffee and banana from the hotel was not going to be enough.

He decided to call her when he stopped for

food and gas. According to the green road sign he had passed a moment earlier, the next exit was only three miles away.

Nick had been listening to the radio all morning, and pressed the scan button on his radio to find something else when a commercial came on.

As he did, he nearly convinced himself he had done something wrong.

The exact same moment, he felt a bump in the right front tire.

Had he run over something?

The steering immediately felt different... heavier somehow... and the car began to pull to the right.

"Terrific," he thought, sarcastically.

He checked his mirror and pulled to the shoulder of the interstate and walked around the car, and there it was.

The front passenger tire was almost completely flat.

He sighed loudly to himself and got back inside the driver's seat, then reached for his phone to call AAA.

After typing in his membership number, he described his predicament and gave the woman on the line his best guess about his vehicle's location.

She said to sit tight. Someone would be

there soon.

Nick put down his phone, shook his head, and breathed out slowly through his nose in disbelief.

As he did, his eyes fell again on the scroll he had found the day before.

The Explorer was sitting safely on the shoulder, but still rocked a bit as cars whizzed by him on the interstate.

He opened up the scroll and read through the list again.

According to the paper, the next commandment was to respect the clock and the calendar. He smiled, convinced that he could now predict the future.

Nick was almost certain he knew what was about to happen.

The tow truck guy would show up early. He would do whatever he needed to with the tire, and then when asked he would explain how his best teammate was somebody who was always on time.

A moment later, he decided he might as well use the next few minutes of waiting constructively, so he grabbed his phone again.

According to the screen, it was 9:26.

He didn't want to, but figured he should call his sister to check on dad.

Nick touched the screen a few times, and

then heard it ringing.

"Hello?"

"Hi, Abs. It's me."

"Morning, Nick. I was just thinking about you." She said the last part with a very peculiar tone.

"Well, you won't believe the day I'm having," he told her.

There was silence on the other end, so he continued.

"I'm sitting on the side of the highway with a flat tire. Have to wait on AAA to send somebody out here to take care of it. Not even on the road three hours and now I'm stuck!"

"That's too bad," his sister responded. "So, are you even curious about dad?"

"Did you get my text?" He asked.

"Huh?" she replied. "Oh... yeah. I got it. But you need to get here, Nick. It's tough for us to do it all, you know?"

Nick held the phone away from his ear a moment and breathed.

"I hear you, sis. I'll get there in a few days, okay? Really. But I'm sitting here with a flat and I can't go anywhere right now. After I get settled in Baltimore, I promise I'll come down to help out."

Silence. Then, "Alright. He's sleeping now," she told him. "I'll tell him you called."

"Thanks again, sis."

"Thanks aren't always enough, Nick." She was angry. Exasperated.

"Okay. I hear you. I'll call you in a few days."

"Bye, Nick." She said – and then he heard her hang up.

He sat in the truck, annoyed. Didn't she get that he was just too busy right now?

He checked the time on his phone. It was 9:31.

A moment later he got a text. But it wasn't from his sister.

It said: "Hey. I'm your tow guy. Be there in a little while."

But the message ended up not being very accurate. By the time the tow truck arrived, it was 10:32.

Nick was infuriated as he jumped out and stomped toward the front of his Explorer to meet the tow guy, who had pulled the flatbed truck in front of and then backed up close enough to load the vehicle there on the side of the highway.

It had been more than a little while. He had been waiting almost an hour!

"Dude – I've been here for an hour!"

The tow guy had already started hooking up chains. He moved slowly and deliberately, without much concern for Nick or his emotion.

He was a large, top-heavy guy wearing a stained white baseball cap with his towing company name on the front and he had on a short sleeved work shirt, untucked.

"Had to grab something to eat. Been running crazy since five am." he muttered, without facing Nick to have any type of conversation.

"You can hop into the cab," he continued, pointing to the front of the tow truck as he held a lever down and watched the motor drag Nick's Explorer onto the flatbed. "I'll get you to the shop, and they can take care of you there."

Nick considered saying something more, but only shook his head in an attempt to convey his displeasure.

Minutes later, the guy was climbing into the driver's seat.

"Name's J.J." he said. "Where you headed?"

"Nowhere fast," Nick said, still annoyed.

J.J. seemed unbothered, and just drove.

Nick looked at his watch. "Any idea how long it might take?"

"I'm just the tow guy. They'll tell you at the shop after they take a look at it."

"I'm just in a hurry. Have to get to Baltimore today."

"Well," J. J. shrugged. "Guess you can talk to the service guy. I don't give much thought about time. I get you there when I get there. Never liked wearing a watch, and I'm not changing."

Nick was in disbelief. Did this guy ever stop to think about somebody other than himself?

Nick sat quietly for a few minutes. This was definitely not what he had expected. J.J. couldn't apparently care less about clocks and calendars.

Then Nick remembered his promise.

"Okay... this is a little weird, but I'd like to ask you a question."

"Alright..." J. J. drawled.

"I'm only asking because I promised somebody I would..." Nick explained. "So, who would you say is the best teammate you ever had?"

J. J.'s shoulders both bounced in amusement at the question.

"That's an easy one. The best teammate I've ever had is me."

"Really? Why do you say that?" Nick probed.

"Always been a lone wolf..." J. J. said. "Don't really get along with people. That's why I do what I do."

Nick didn't ask any follow up questions. He just sat there watching the road and wondering how long this detour would end up taking him.

A few minutes later, he had another thought. In a way, he was a little like the tow truck guy. As he thought back to his last two jobs, and even his conversations with his sister and how he treated his family, he realized that he hadn't thought of their needs at all.

The bump from the tow truck hitting a curb snapped him out of his internal dialogue.

As they pulled into the repair shop parking lot, J. J. spoke again and interrupted Nick's contemplation.

"If I had to choose somebody else, it'd be my dog."

"What's that?" Nick said.

The tow truck came to a stop in the open area on the right side of a large metal building that had two garage doors and a door that probably opened into the office to the left of them.

J.J. was staring out the driver's side window, not making eye contact.

"My dog. Clara." J. J. said. "Never known anybody as dependable as her. Doesn't matter what day it is or how frustrated I am. She jumps on the couch with me and looks up and puts her paw on my leg."

He patted his thigh, as if seeing her there.

"She's always there when I need her. Happy to see me…"

"Dogs just have a sense about them." Nick nodded, still uncomfortable, but trying to mirror the guy's sentiment.

"Yeah." J. J. grabbed the steering wheel tightly with his right hand as he leaned toward the door. "Not like most people."

He got out of the truck and walked over to the office. On the glass door Nick saw the same "Elite Auto Repair" logo that was on J. J.'s dirty baseball cap.

What a surprising answer, Nick thought.

This had been a weird trip. Completely different than what he had anticipated.

When he got to the office of the repair shop, he was greeted by a younger guy with shaggy hair down to his neck, wearing a dark blue company and faded jeans.

"Hi Mr. Turner," he said. "I'll be working on your car. J. J. says that your tire can't be patched, so we'll probably need to get you a couple of new ones."

"Two?" Nick asked, incredulous.

"Yes, sir. With your tread worn down a bit, you can't put a new one on next to an old one like that. But we'll put the new ones on front for you and you'll be fine. We can get the same brand for you. Shouldn't take more than a couple hours to get 'em here and mount 'em."

Nick couldn't believe it. He felt like he

would never get to Baltimore.

He was not happy about having to pay for two tires... He wanted to talk to Coach Watkins again. And he was very hungry.

"Alright." Nick said, reluctantly. "Do what you have to, I guess."

The mechanic nodded. "I've got your contact information. If you want to get lunch, I'll call you when it's done."

Nick walked out of the office to look for places to eat. There were a few fast food places on either side of the same street, and he quickly decided on Zaxby's.

It looked about a hundred yards away, so he started walking.

The day was warm, but overcast, and he kept his eyes on the ground in front of him.

As he walked, he pulled his phone out of his front pocket and pressed the screen a few times.

"Nicky!"

"Coach, you won't believe the conversations I've had," Nick announced.

"Well," Coach Watkins' gravelly voice replied, "Maybe that's a good thing. Tell me what's been happening since yesterday..."

Nick took a deep breath, then explained.

"Okay. Last time we talked, I told you how the people I talked to were giving me answers that matched that list you gave us, right?"

"You did," he agreed.

"So, after we talked, it kept on the same way! I met the owner of a hotel who talked to me about staying coachable... and a bartender told me to be aware of and encourage others. Then this morning a lady told me how important it is to always do more than is expected!"

Nick veered into the Zaxby's parking lot and kept walking toward the door.

Coach Watkins hadn't responded.

"It's so weird. Right down the list, you know?"

Coach Watkins just said "Yep," then went quiet again.

"But then... today... I get a flat tire. And I know the tow truck guy is gonna talk to me about being on time and respecting the calendar, right?" Nick continued. "But he didn't! He showed up late and couldn't have cared less about clocks or calendars. Really made me mad... I just now got to the repair shop!"

"Well, that IS interesting," Coach said.

"Yeah... so, uh..." Nick's rant was quickly running out of steam.

"Nicky," Coach interjected, "sometimes you learn from people what not to do. Everybody you meet can share a valuable lesson... especially when you ask a good question or two...

but not every teacher has the same style."

Now Nick was the silent one.

"It's like parents," Coach Watkins explained. "Some are great examples of what you want to do when you have kids. The others are great examples of what you should never want to do. But both are good teachers."

He paused to let Nick digest the idea.

"Sounds like your tow truck guy did share a lesson on respecting the clock and the calendar. Just not how you expected him to..."

Nick realized that maybe Coach was right.

"Hey, Coach... didn't you talk a lot to us about being on time? About being early?" Nick asked, thinking back to his time as an athlete.

"Well, I probably did."

"So you really think it's one of the most important things a teammate can do?"

"It's in the top ten," Coach answered.

Nick walked into the restaurant and found a seat. The air conditioning felt good. He decided to wait and order after he finished his conversation with Coach.

"Why, though?" he asked. "I mean, I wasn't always early, but how did that hurt us?"

"How did it feel this morning?" Coach asked.

"What?"

"When he was late. When you were waiting,"

Coach said. "How did it feel?"

"Oh. Well… I got angry."

"Why?"

"'Cause he wasn't thinking about me!" Nick said, remembering his annoyance.

"Exactly." Coach said.

Nick waited for him to elaborate.

"Nicky… if you are thinking about others, if you are respecting them, you will respect the clock because you value their time as much as your own. But it isn't just that…"

He let Nick consider the first part for a few seconds.

"The even more important part of respecting the clock is realizing that it keeps moving. It's not just about respecting others' time and being early to meetings," he said. "That is important… but it's also important to remember that your time is valuable."

Okay… what do you mean by that, though?" Nick asked.

"I mean you don't get it back. Wherever you are, you need to be there. Be where your feet are. Think about how valuable each day is." Coach Watkins paused and then coughed before finishing his thought. "You only get so many of them. So whatever you're doing, don't just show up to endure it. You should show up to enjoy it."

Nick recalled one of the sayings Coach had shared so often in their locker room.

"Hustlers hate slackers, and slackers hate hustlers, right?" He asked.

"Right, Nicky. If you respect the clock and the calendar, you won't waste time. People who value time can't stand people who don't."

"Okay, Coach. I think I got it. But here's the thing," Nick explained, curiously. "It's already been 24 hours... and I haven't gotten to the end of the list yet..."

"Well, Nicky, to get what you really want, you might sometimes need to do more than you first expected." Coach answered. "Give me a call if you find a way to get the last three, okay?"

"Yeah, Coach... Thanks." Nick said. And Coach hung up on his end.

Nick exhaled and collected his thoughts.

He had three more commandments to get to somehow.

He figured he needed to keep asking his question to see if he could finish what he started. But first he needed to eat.

CHAPTER 9

know your role and contribute your strengths

Zaxby's wasn't very busy yet, but it was still before noon.

Nick ordered a chicken finger plate, filled his cup with lots of ice and sweet tea, and went back to the same table he had been sitting at while on the phone.

Then it rang again.

"Hello?"

"Mr. Turner?"

"Yes?"

"Hi, this is Melanie, from The Munsey up in Baltimore… I need to confirm that these men are your movers. There is a man named Jack here?"

"Thanks, sorry about that. Yes… you can

let them into the apartment with my stuff..."

Nick couldn't' believe he had overlooked that! After the deposit and lease and everything else, he had neglected to inform them of the movers coming today.

"No problem, sir."

"Thank you," Nick said. "I should be there by this evening."

"See you then, sir," she said, and then hung up.

He shook his head, then took a deep breath to collect himself. What a crazy day.

He would have normally just sat there at the restaurant, with time to kill while waiting for tires. But following the conversation with Coach Watkins, he felt like he needed to do something useful with the time he had.

But he had nothing to work on from his job. He would be starting there tomorrow.

And he really wasn't eager to call his sister back yet.

So he ate. And he looked around at the other customers.

And soon he reached again for his phone. He scrolled first through his Twitter and then through his Facebook account, reading the posts and updates.

One of the updates on Facebook was a picture of Wayne, one of the guys that worked with Nick at his previous job.

Wayne was a good guy, and had always seemed to like him.

After the education he had gotten from strangers he had spoken to over the last day or so, Nick thought it would be interesting to hear from somebody he knew.

He dipped his last bite of chicken in the Zax sauce, chewed and swallowed impatiently, wiped his hands on a napkin, and scrolled through his list of contacts until he reached Wayne Miller.

He thought it would be best to text first. "Hey, man. Just checking in. Give me a call if you can!"

Nick pressed send and grabbed his cup to drink a sip of his sweet tea.

His phone rang before he could put it back on the table.

"Nick! How are things in Baltimore, my man?" Wayne asked, with an energetic voice.

"Hey, Wayne. Thanks for calling back so quick!" Nick adjusted himself in the seat and noticed the restaurant was beginning to fill up with customers. "You won't believe what happened... I'm not even there yet. Got a flat and I'm waiting to get a couple tires here just outside Richmond, I think..."

"Aw, man. Too bad. Flat tires are a lot like

bad attitudes... right? Can't get very far If you have one! So, anything I can do?" Wayne asked, concerned.

"Actually. Yeah. Not with the tires, but maybe with the attitude."

"How can I help?" he asked.

Nick paused to try and explain it the best he could.

"Okay, so I've been thinking a lot about what it was like working with me. And the more I think back on how I was, the more I see that I may not have been the best teammate."

"Nobody's perfect, Nick" Wayne said, trying to be kind.

"Yeah, I get that. But I'm thinking there were a bunch of things I could have done better if I had thought about it. So I wanted to ask you a question."

"Sure... no problem," Wayne replied. "What's the question?"

"Okay... I just want to know... who is the best teammate you ever had?"

"Hmmm," Wayne said, thinking. "Tough question, man. I've worked with some really good people."

Part of Nick was hoping Wayne would throw him a bone of minor recognition.

That didn't happen, though.

"I know!" Wayne said, excited. "And you'll

like this one, since you played ball too! Back in high school we had a guy on our team named Bryce. Real hard working kid. But he was only like five foot nothing, you know?"

"Okay…" Nick prompted him to go on. The restaurant was getting louder as more people came in for lunch, so he held the phone closer to his ear.

"So Bryce was a great defensive player. He was terrific on the ball, getting steals and stuff. But he couldn't shoot the ball at all, you know? Never put in the time to get his form right. So one day we are watching film and coach gives everybody a copy of the team stats. And he's talking about who needs to cut down on turnovers and who needs to get more deflections. And then he stops the tape after Bryce took a three."

Nick had a pretty good idea what was about to happen next in his story, but didn't add any comment.

"And so coach holds up his copy of the team stats," Wayne continued, "and stands right next to Bryce and asks him in front of everybody, 'Now Bryce… how many threes have you made this season so far?"

"None, right?" Nick guessed.

"Exactly. None. So coach asks him another question. He says, 'Alright, Bryce. How many offensive rebounds have you gotten this season?'"

"None again?" Nick said.

"Right. None. So coach asks him what he thinks he needs to work on to earn more playing time, right? And Bryce is just a sophomore and he's nervous, so he spits out his answer without really thinking. He says, 'threes and rebounds, coach?'"

Wayne laughed out loud over the phone.

"That's funny," Nick admitted.

"Yeah. So coach explains to him that those two things were most definitely not what he should be focused on. He says that the thing Bryce did best was pressuring the ball – and if he wanted to play more he needed to do more of what he did well, you know?"

"Yeah. I get it." Nick said. "So why was he the best teammate you ever had?"

"Oh... well, because he did what coach said," Wayne answered. "He was always positive, and he worked hard... and he kept good enough grades to get into a D3 school and play, I think. But after that, I've never seen anybody who did a better job of knowing who he was and giving his team what it needed."

One of the Zaxby's employees came by Nick's table and offered to carry his trash away, but he waved them off. He was enjoying his talk with Wayne.

"Guess I wasn't always that guy?" Nick asked, a bit apologetically.

"You know, Nick, our business is a lot like basketball," Wayne said. "I mean, everybody on our team goes into a new project knowing what part of it they are responsible for – what they do well... but in the heat of the game, when something comes up, sometimes you have to be willing to step up and do what the team needs."

Nick grabbed a napkin and started playing with it in his other hand.

He stared over the table into the empty seat across from him, and tried to wrap his mind around what Wayne was trying to say.

"Don't think I follow you," Nick admitted.

"You ever heard of tessellations?" Wayne asked.

Nick shook his head, then answered. "No?"

"A tessellation," Wayne explained, "is a repeated pattern of shapes, one beside the next, with no gaps. There's an artist – his name is M.C. Escher. He's famous for some of his drawings that use them. But it can also be something as simple as an arrangement of different tiles on a bathroom floor."

Nick was listening, but didn't interrupt.

"So, here's why it is important." Wayne explained. "See, for a team to accomplish its goals, you have to be willing to adapt to the personalities and talent around you, 'cause a team is like…" Wayne paused. "A team is like a bunch of different sized puzzle pieces, you know? And, yeah, you have to know what you do well… but you also have to look around and see what's going on around you…"

"And I didn't ever do that, did I?" Nick admitted.

"I think you were just focused on your job. And that's good. You did a good job with your stuff. I mean, you're a talented guy," Wayne reminded him.

"But?" Nick prompted him.

"But sometimes you could have done a better job filling the gaps in our tessellation," Wayne said. "You know, you just seemed kind of distant most of the time… and you were focused on your stuff, which was good – but then people would think that you didn't see the big picture… that you didn't care about things that they needed help with, sometimes."

"Wow," Nick said. "No, I mean… thanks. I need to hear that. It's helpful."

He wadded up the napkin and put it on his tray, then sat back in the booth.

"I appreciate you telling me," Nick said. He was sincere.

"Yeah, sure man. Maybe that's just been your way, you know?"

"Yeah, maybe," Nick said weakly.

"But you can always change, you know?" Wayne said, enthusiastically. "You don't have to do things that way in Baltimore, right? I mean, you can be different…"

Wayne paused to consider his next example.

"Think about it like this, man. A lot of people want to win, but only on their terms. I mean, how many great players never won a championship because their ego wouldn't allow them to become a small part of something bigger?"

Nick wasn't connecting the dots.

"See, man, if you know your strengths, and if you know your teammates, you can do what you do well and fill in the gaps in the tessellation!"

"What do you mean, if I know my teammates?" Nick asked. He had always done his job well. Yes, there were other people involved in the project that he needed to communicate with at times, and there were deadlines, and there were issues that popped up… but he was focused on just doing his job.

Maybe that was the problem.

"I mean, as a teammate, part of my role is to know more than my role. To work better with others, you have to know who you're working with, right?" Wayne clarified. "Their problems… their passions… their personalities.

Then you can do your job better and fill in the gaps. And they can fill in yours… you know? I mean, did you ever ask anybody in our project team to go out for a meal, or to grab a cup of coffee?" Wayne asked.

"People notice that stuff… and I think they feel like part of your role on a team is to connect with the people on it…"

Nick hadn't taken the time to get to know anything but his role.

All the way back to high school, he had known his strengths, but he had never thought about getting to know his teammates better or filling in gaps or tessellations…

There had been a long silence on the phone, and finally Nick filled it.

"Thanks, Wayne," Nick said.

"Yeah, sure. Probably a lot more than you wanted to hear, right?" Wayne said, lightening the mood.

"No, uh… I really appreciate it," Nick responded. "I needed to hear it. Helps me to understand some other stuff I've been hearing from people…"

"Alright, man. Good to hear from you." Wayne said.

"Okay, yeah. Let's stay in touch," Nick said. "And Wayne?"

"Yeah?"

"I've been thinking about it the last day or so. And when I ask myself the question, it's your name that keeps coming up as my best teammate... Thanks for talking to me."

"Yeah... anytime, man."

"Okay," Nick said.

"Take care, Nick," Wayne said. And they hung up.

CHAPTER 10

prioritize team goals ahead of personal gains

The guy came by again to grab his tray.

He was about Nick's age, wearing a black baseball cap with the Zaxby's logo across the front in white, with tan pants and a blue short sleeve button down shirt.

The guy was clearly a good worker, and had been busy talking with customers and cleaning off tables the entire time Nick had been talking on the phone with Wayne.

Nick said "thank you" and watched the cleaning guy carry it over to the trash can.

He sat back in the booth again, collecting his thoughts.

Eight down, two to go.

He didn't have the paper to refer to. It

was still in the Explorer, so he couldn't remember the last two commandments he hadn't yet heard about... but he knew there were two more lessons remaining to finish the list of ten.

And the only way to learn was to ask the question.

So Nick looked around for the cleaning guy... but couldn't find him.

As he scanned the restaurant, Nick saw another employee straightening up the condiments and napkins counter. She looked like a high school kid, with her light brown hair in a ponytail, and she smiled warmly at the customers that were waiting on food or refilling their drinks. Her uniform was the same as the one the first guy had on, except for the hat.

Sitting near the door, his booth was only a few feet away and he was able to raise his hand to get her attention when she turned.

"Yes, sir... can I get you something?" she asked, warmly.

"Hi, my name is Nick." He said.

She smiled, waiting for his request.

"I, uh... really don't need anything. But I do have a question." He stated.

The girl looked a bit unsure about his request, but her politeness kept her there. Her smile grew more thin, but she was courteous with her reply.

"Alright."

She adjusted her stance and clasped her hands behind her back, ready for his question.

"So, I've been asking a lot of people the same thing the last couple of days, and I'd like to hear your answer. Who is the best teammate you ever had?"

She laughed, her top teeth showing above her lower lip.

"Really?" she asked.

"Yeah... really. Think about it" Nick encouraged her, looking serious.

"Oh... I don't play any sports," she said. She shrugged her shoulders, said "sorry," and began to turn her attention back to work.

"No, wait..." Nick pleaded. "What about here? Who is the best teammate you have had here, and why?" he asked, hoping she would give it enough consideration to provide a quality answer.

She turned to look at the order counter, where people were standing at registers, and then her eyes seemed to go further back, to where the kitchen staff was cooking and preparing the meals.

After a few seconds, she turned back around to face him.

"You mean... who I like the most?"

"Kind of..." Nick said. "I mean, who is the

best person to work with? Who does the stuff you wish everybody else would do?"

"Oh..." She nodded her head in understanding. "That'd be Allen," and she pointed to the other side of the restaurant, where the cleaning guy was leaning over another table, wiping it down.

"He's always doing stuff to help us out."

"Like cleaning?" Nick asked. He assumed that most people wouldn't like that job.

"Yeah. But he does it all. And he doesn't really have to... I mean, he's the manager... but he makes it feel like... like we all have the same job," she said.

That sounded interesting. "What do you mean, 'the same job?'" Nick asked.

"In our shift meetings," she explained. "It's what he always says. 'We're all here to do the same job - Make our store special by making our customers feel special.'"

Nick wanted to talk to him.

He said thank you to the girl, and she happily went back to busying herself.

Then he walked over to a recently vacated table, where the cleaning guy was working on getting everything ready for the next guests to use. Allen was genuinely engaged in doing a good job of it.

"Hey, Allen?" Nick held out his hand.

Allen turned around, a bit startled. He put down the spray bottle of sanitizer he was holding and shook Nick's hand. "Yes, sir! How can I help you?"

"Well," Nick said to him, "one of your people told me that you are the best teammate they ever had... and I was curious about how you did that."

Allen was obviously not prepared for his question.

"Well... that's nice to hear..." he said. "but I don't really do anything special."

"She said you say something to them each day in your meetings?" Nick mentioned.

Allen squinted, cocking his chin to one side as he thought, then raised his eyebrows and said "the same job thing?"

"Yeah," Nick replied. "Can you talk more about that?"

Allen motioned for him to sit down at the table they were standing beside.

"Sure."

They settled into the chairs across from one another.

"A lot of times, people work next to each other but they're really just focused on themselves. They think about their own paycheck, and they don't really care about how the business is doing, because it doesn't affect them.

You know what I mean?"

Nick nodded, realizing that he had been one of those guys.

"So, my dad owns a few other businesses. And he had seen that, too. So when he decided to put me in charge of this location, he had me sign a contract to pay me minimum wage for the first year." Allen paused for a moment.

"But after the first year, if our store was in the top twenty-five percent of earnings, nation-wide, according to the contract I'd become an equal partner and get fifty percent of the business…"

"Sounds like a pretty good deal!" Nick commented.

"Right." Allen agreed.

"So how is the store doing? How many months before your year is up?" Nick asked, growing more curious.

"Well, the store's been doing great. We've been in the top five percent of sales and customer satisfaction for the last eight months in a row."

"That's awesome," Nick said, excited for him. "So how long until your ownership kicks in?"

Allen smiled. "That was about six months ago."

Nick's forehead wrinkled.

"Wait…" Nick asked, not yet grasping

the idea. "I thought you said that you became owner after the first year. Why are you still cleaning tables?"

Around them, a steady stream of customers continued to enter and eat and leave.

Allen must have trusted his staff, as he didn't look concerned about taking a few minutes to talk. He gave Nick his full attention.

"I decided it was important to keep doing the same thing that made us successful to begin with," he answered.

"Cleaning?" Nick said, half jokingly.

"Thinking about the store, not just myself." Allen said. He meant it. "I only benefitted if the store did well, right? But because I knew that, I made sure the store did well. I didn't think about fairness or recognition or even my paycheck — because I knew that if the team was successful, my success would follow."

"Scoreboard, not scorebook..." Nick mumbled to himself.

"What's that?" Allen asked him.

"Something my coach used to say to us back in high school. He wanted scoreboard guys, not scorebook guys."

Allen didn't understand, and it was Nick's turn to do some explaining.

"Okay, in basketball, some guys have a habit of running over to check the scorebook...

They want to know how many points they scored. Or they check the stat sheet to see how many rebounds or assists they got..." Nick could hear Watkins saying it as if he were back in the locker room hearing it the first time.

"But those guys will kill you, because they're just interested in themselves. Coach wanted us to be scoreboard guys. He said the most important stat at the end of the game was the score. If we contributed to a win, and if we learned something and got better, he said it was a good game."

Nick felt something inside him click.

The words weren't just empty speeches that he had endured. They really were useful nuggets of information.

That list of commandments that Coach had given him so many years ago weren't just about being a better athlete.

They were about being a better person.

"You got it..." Allen agreed. "That's it exactly!" he said. "I tell them we're all here to do the same job... to make our store special by making our customers feel special... because I really believe it. If everybody sees the big picture, they stop feeling like employees and they start feeling more like owners themselves."

"That makes sense," Nick said, considering the idea.

It was another example of something he hadn't done in the past.

Another example of something he needed to do.

"I think it would have been selfish of me to think of myself differently. I can't give a roller coaster of effort based on what I like doing or how I am feeling. So I always put the team goals ahead of my own personal gain... and it turns out that was the key to our success."

"I like that phrase, 'roller coaster of effort'" Nick said. "My old coach used to say he wanted to know what he was getting when he pushed our button as players. He said the worst thing you could do is be a roller coaster..."

Nick looked around the restaurant again, and remembered his tires.

"Yeah... Managers and employees are same way." Allen said. "They want to know that they can depend on you to be there and care about the team more than yourself. That's why I do what I do..."

He got up and grabbed his bottle of sanitizer, ready to jump back into action.

"If the store is successful, then I'll be successful."

"A rising tide lifts all ships, right?" Nick echoed.

"Right!" Allen said. "Have a great day, sir.

Enjoyed talking with you! Hope you can come back soon."

Nick waved as Allen smiled and left the booth.

Three tables over, he watched Allen pick up a few pieces of trash to carry it away, then wipe down the table for the next guest.

Nick headed to the restroom before going back over to the repair shop.

Hopefully the tires would be ready soon.

CHAPTER 11

claim personal responsibility for results

Not long after he returned, they had the two new tires balanced and mounted on the front of his vehicle.

Nick paid the bill with his credit card and was on the road again.

It was just before two o'clock in the afternoon.

He checked directions on his phone, and convinced himself that, with any luck, he could still make it to his new apartment by six.

He had a new job to start tomorrow and wanted to get some rest.

He was also anxious to see the job that Rich and Jack had done with getting everything set up in his new apartment.

He glanced at the box of items beside him on the passenger seat a few times, but didn't reach for the rolled up list that had been such a huge part of his last two days.

Nick just wanted to think.

As he drove, he reviewed in his mind the lessons that others had shared with him since he began his trip.

Have fun and stay positive... Give and request clear expectations... Frequently share appreciation and thanks... Continue to grow and stay coachable... Be aware of and encourage others... Do more than is expected with enthusiasm... Respect the clock and the calendar... Know your role and contribute your strengths... Put team goals ahead of personal gains...

As he thought about each of them, he realized that he had not been a very good teammate for the people that knew him.

And he still had one more lesson. He would wait to call coach until after he had that conversation.

The trip was relatively uneventful the rest of the way.

Other than experiencing heavier traffic through D. C. than he would have expected and a little difficulty finding a few good radio stations along the way, he had not had any problems traveling the rest of the way to his new city.

It was 5:17 when Nick arrived at his new apartment building. It was a historic structure in the heart of the city that would be convenient to everything.

He was able to park in the basement garage, and chose to leave his bags and boxes in the Explorer for now and make his way up to the lobby.

As he exited the elevator, he was impressed with the marbled floors and dark wood trim and elegant furniture in the lobby. The scene more than exceeded the expectations that online images had given him after doing a few online searches and reading the building's reviews.

He found a woman standing at the leasing office desk behind a computer, and walked over to her.

"Welcome to The Munsey!" she said.

"Hi," he answered. "My name is Nick Turner. I was scheduled to move in earlier today?"

"Right." Her eyes opened wide with recognition. "I'm Melanie. We've talked on the phone a few times…"

"Oh yeah… right! Nice to meet you," Nick said.

"You too," she replied. I've got everything

taken care of for you. Let me get you your keys..." She turned to retrieve an envelope that was lying on another desk, on top of some papers.

She brought back the envelope and the papers and placed them in front of him.

"Here you go... we just need to have you sign a couple things, if you don't mind." She typed a few things and glanced at the computer screen again.

"Looks like most everything else has been taken care of already... but this afternoon was a bit of a surprise!"

She handed him a pen.

"This afternoon?" Nick asked, looking at the papers.

"Oh, yes sir... Your movers. They were terrific... but the service elevator had been reserved by another resident. We figured it out, though!" she explained. "Just a speed bump!"

Melanie had terrific energy, and struck him as a charismatic young lady.

She was not very tall, but carried herself with confidence and an infectious smile. Her eyes were large and brown and cheerful.

"So what happened?" Nick asked, genuinely concerned.

"It wasn't anything major... but since the other resident had the key to our service elevator, your stuff was going to have to wait until they brought it back, or have to go up six flights of stairs..."

"Aw, man." Nick was upset at his oversight.

"Yeah... luckily I was able to get in touch, and they were willing to postpone their movers a couple of hours to let Jack use the elevator for your stuff. I think your guys had to make their last few trips up the stairs, but they got it all taken care of... no worries!"

"Wow," Nick said, gratefully. "You are amazing."

"Wow," she smiled back. "You are observant!"

He laughed, began to leave, then caught himself.

There was still one more commandment from the list that he hadn't been introduced to. Maybe she was the one to share it.

"Could I ask you a really weird question?" he asked, realizing that he was still holding her pen in his hand.

"Depends on the question," she said, lifting her eyebrows and then flashing a wry grin.

"Okay, great." Nick said, and leaned over to put the pen back on her desk.

He paused before continuing.

"So, who would you say is the best team-mate you ever had?"

"What a surprising question!" She declared.

She clasped her hands in front of her, biting her tongue and looking up to her left while she thought a moment. Then she exhaled.

"I would have to say... my dad," she answered.

Nick waited for her to elaborate, but she didn't do so immediately.

"Okay... why?" he prompted.

"Well, I've been lucky enough to have a lot of good teammates." She lingered on that thought, remembering.

"First when I played volleyball, back in school. And even now, in my job. I've worked with really good people... But my dad was special." She looked up before finishing. "And he's probably the reason you got your furniture upstairs today!"

"Is that right?" Nick responded.

"Yes, sir. Really."

"I'm not still a sir, am I?" he corrected her, feeling more of a connection.

She smiled, polite and still professional.

"He was a Marine. He was always strong... a protector. But more than anything else, he taught me to be responsible... that I needed to find a way to make something work if it was important. He didn't believe in making excuses, you know?"

Melanie looked at him for agreement, which he gave with a sincere nod.

"You know... I really did think about him earlier today. It was a story he told me that I always remember. It reminded me to fix the problem."

"So now you have to tell me the story" Nick said. He sat down in one of the leather chairs nearby.

"Are you sure?" she asked, a bit sheepishly.

"Definitely."

"Right. Okay... well Dad only told it to me once, in middle school, but after I heard it I starting to see exactly what he meant. And he'd call people reporters or doctors when we were out sometimes, so it was something I never forgot..."

Nick looked up at her from his chair. She was talking with her hands, and as he watched her he noticed that she was very attractive.

"So..." she said, "he told me to imagine that we were out driving on vacation... on a secluded mountain road. The air is clean and clear. There's a view of a big beautiful lake through the trees. It's a nice warm sunny day. And your favorite song is playing on the radio..."

She looked over to make sure he was getting a feel for this perfect scene.

"And as you round the next curve, BOOM

– you get hit by an oncoming car!"

Nick jumped a bit, startled by the sudden violent turn of events in her story.

Melanie grinned to see that part of her story having it's intended impact.

"So your car is thrown off the road and rolls over a couple of times into some trees, and you are there in the driver's seat… and you can feel that you are hurt bad… and you are hoping somebody will see what happened soon and come help."

She was fully engaged in telling the story, and enjoying herself. Nick was following the story, but also enjoyed watching her tell it.

"A few moments later, you are still there, stuck in your car, and you hear a car stop and a voice calls down to you…" Melanie continued. "You hear footsteps moving toward you through the brush… and as soon as he arrives, you breathe a sigh of relief… because he says to you, don't worry – I'm a reporter!"

She snickered, ruining the effect it was supposed to have on him.

"A reporter?" Nick asked.

"I know, right?" she asked. "Who needs that?"

"You don't," he said.

"Exactly. You don't need a reporter. But when some people see a problem, all they do is point at it and announce it to others."

Nick understood.

But then Melanie kept talking.

"So imagine you're in that same predicament. And the guy walks down toward your car. and as soon as he arrives, he says to you, don't worry – I'm a lawyer!"

Nick didn't say anything, waiting for her to explain this one.

"See, you don't need a lawyer either – but when some people see a problem, all they do is look to blame somebody else. Like a lawyer identifying who is guilty, you know?" she said.

"Okay..." Nick said, understanding.

"What my dad wanted me to get, is that when something is wrong, you need a doctor. When a doctor sees a problem, all they think about doing is jumping in and getting their hands dirty and working to fix it. They don't care about excuses. They don't care about blame. They care about the person who needs help, you know?"

Nick liked this girl.

"If you see a piece of trash in the hallway, you don't walk past it or blame it on somebody else... you just pick it up," he said.

"Right." She said. "People who are responsible know that pointing and blaming are a waste of time. Excuses are a waste of time.

Problems don't get better because you point at them or blame somebody else... they get better when you take responsibility to fix them!"

Nick nodded, amused and impressed with her passion.

"Dad was the best teammate I ever had, because he taught me to claim personal responsibility for results. And he taught me a great question that I always ask when I am part of something that should have gone better. Instead of making excuses, I ask myself, 'what part of my leadership was responsible for that result?'"

"I like that," he said.

"Yeah... me too," she admitted.

Claiming personal responsibility for results was the last commandment on the list, and it was the one he figured that he had needed to hear the most.

Back in high school, everything had been somebody else's fault. Every turnover that was made he would complain about. Every time the other team scored he instead of taking responsibility himself for talking more and making others better.

And at his last two jobs, it had been the same thing.

Nothing was his fault. When things took longer than they should have... when issues popped up in the system... he had been a reporter. He had been a lawyer. But he had never been the guy who stepped up and felt accountable.

He had never asked himself, "what part of my leadership was responsible for that result?"

Nick stood up. "That was a good story," he said. "I appreciate you telling it... and thanks for telling me about your dad."

"You're welcome," Melanie replied. "I imagine we'll see each other again, now that you live here."

There was an awkward silence.

"Well, thanks again for helping to get my stuff upstairs! Your dad must have been a good guy..."

Melanie grinned. "Yeah, well, that was definitely from dad. Part of me wanted to point at the rules and blame things I couldn't control for why it wouldn't get done. But dad would have said that was how victims talk."

"So... how did he say winners talk, then?" Nick asked.

"Oh, he'd say that winners know that if you blame somebody else for stuff, your circumstances won't change until they do... but if you claim responsibility, you give yourself the power to change." She shrugged. "I just figured it was easier to find a way to make it work than to explain to you and your movers why it didn't.

It wasn't a brick wall... it was just a speed bump. I knew I could handle it."

"Well, I really do appreciate it." Nick repeated.

His mind was reeling. As he thought more and more about her story, about the lesson, he felt a bit more ashamed of his past behaviors. But in that moment, standing across from Melanie, he also felt just enough courage to ask one more question before he left.

"So... after I get settled in..." he paused, imagining the boxes waiting for him in the car. "Think you might want to go out for a meal, or to grab a cup of coffee?"

"You know," Melanie said. "I just might..."

She flashed a playful smile at him.

Nick smiled back, then walked out of the office and back to the Explorer to begin unloading his things. He had a lot on his mind.

He was thinking about the boxes he needed to carry upstairs.

He was thinking about needing some rest for the new job tomorrow.

But mostly he kept thinking about Melanie's smile.

CHAPTER 12

learn the lesson or relive it

Nick held his phone beside his right ear as he surveyed the living room and kitchen of his new apartment.

He had finished carrying up the boxes that had been in his Explorer, and the box from his passenger seat was sitting on the granite countertop of the kitchen's breakfast bar.

In his left hand was the gift he had just found two days ago.

He was proud of what he had learned, and while there were a number of things he still had to unpack, he was proud of the way his new home now looked.

High ceilings, fresh paint, hardwood floors, great views… and all of his furniture exactly where Jack's diagram had promised. Everything looked terrific.

The phone rang twice before Coach Watkins answered.

"Nicky. How was your trip?"

"Hi Coach. A few unexpected bumps in the road, but it was good. I just wanted to give you a call to let you know I kept asking your question, and now I've heard about all ten of the commandments from your list."

"Well," his voice was like a handsaw cutting through cardboard. "That list wasn't mine, Nicky. I got it years ago from somebody who was a far better coach than me."

"Okay... Well, I just want you to know that I'm grateful to you for giving it to me... for encouraging me to ask the question. I've learned a lot." Nick said, proudly.

"So you start your new job tomorrow?" Coach asked.

"Yes, sir. And I think this one will be a much better experience."

"Why's that?" Coach Watkins prodded.

Nick stared at the window as he answered. "Because I'm different now, I think. Because that question helped me see how much better I can be..."

Coach was quiet.

"But it didn't feel normal... asking people,

I mean…" Nick said.

"Good."

Now Nick was quiet, waiting on an explanation.

"It isn't normal," Coach confirmed. "That's exactly the point."

He cleared his throat before saying more. "You know what normal people do, Nicky? Normal people think of themselves. Normal people live with blinders on… Normal people do just enough to get by. The worst thing you could aspire to be is normal."

Nick never appreciated his talks when he had been in school. Now, after two unexpected days of personal growth, he hung on every word.

"In fact, I'd say that as a player, as a person, as a teammate your job is to be abnormal.

Successful people – achievers – the ones that you heard stories about being winning teammates – they were abnormal. Normal is your enemy."

Nick looked down at the paper as he listened.

"If you want to be like everybody else," Coach said, "if you are aiming for mediocrity – you won't ever stand out. That's normal. But if you truly want to live a life that you're proud of – if you want to have a positive impact on people around you – winning teammates are abnormal..."

"Okay, Coach. I got it. I know." Nick said.

"That ain't enough," Coach said, resolutely.

"What do you mean?"

"I mean that knowing ain't enough," Coach explained. "It's good that you know the list now... I'm glad you know... but knowing and doing are further apart than two sides of the Grand Canyon. And if all you do is know something, you won't see much around you change. Life has a way of teaching you the same thing over and over until you do things different. You either learn the lesson or you relive it."

Nick knew he was right.

He hadn't learned to be a winning teammate in school, so he kept reliving the same lesson at his first two jobs. He was determined that he wouldn't relive it again. He would learn to do things differently.

He had always just seen himself as an employee... he thought the team's success was somebody else's job. Now he understood that winning teammates saw themselves as owners, not employees.

"Okay, Coach. I'll do things differently. Really."

"Well, good. Then let me ask you another question," Coach said.

"Okay…" Nick leaned against the kitchen counter and breathed.

"Nicky, over the last day or two you learned that great teammates are great noticers. You only see what you train yourself to look for. Your eyes see what your questions ask them to. Right?"

"Yes, sir."

"Well, hopefully you see now that life is a team sport. The world doesn't revolve around you. And to be a winning teammate, you have to stop asking what you can get, and start asking what you can give…"

"Yes, sir?"

Nick wondered if there was a question coming soon.

"So here is my question, Nicky. How many people," he asked, "would say that YOU were the best teammate they ever had?"

The question left Nick silent…

"Because that's how you measure impact," Coach stated. "That's success."

Nick knew he was right. He really was getting it.

And he realized he did still have a lot of work to do… not just to be better at his job tomorrow, but to be better with other people in his life as well.

"Thanks, Coach. I understand." Nick said.

"I'll be in touch, okay? And thanks again for the list. You really changed my life."

"Good, Nicky. Talk soon, then…" Coach said, and then the phone was dead.

But Nick did not put the phone down.

Instead he pressed the screen a few times and returned the phone to his right ear.

It rang three times, but then he heard someone pick up.

"Hello?"

"Hey, Abs. It's me," Nick said. He waited to hear her reaction, but was determined to stay positive regardless. She deserved that.

"Hey Nick," she said, halfheartedly. "What's up?"

"I just want you to know that I know I've been a bad brother. A bad son. You and your husband have been terrific, and I've been a complete slug."

She didn't say anything.

"I just wanted to call… to let you know I'll be there this weekend to see dad. And I'll drive down early, to be there by lunchtime. And I'm really sorry that I didn't take more responsibility for helping out. But I will now. Not just with you, but with everything. I know why I lost my last job and why I lost my last girlfriend and why our team didn't do as well as it should have way back in high school… and I know this sounds crazy, but I'll explain more when we have a chance to talk."

He finally stopped rambling and took a breath, but his sister was quiet on the other end of the phone.

"I know you have to get the kids to bed and stuff... I had a really weird trip on the way up here, Abbie... but I really needed it. And I am going to be a better teammate. So... Is Saturday okay?"

"Um..." she stammered. "Yeah, Nick... Saturday would be great..."

"Okay, then," he said, proud of himself. He imagined the surprised look on her face.

"Nick... you..." she stammered. "You don't know what that would mean to us!"

Was she crying?

"Dad's dementia... it's exhausting. I didn't know how to tell you... but it would be so nice... to have you here... even for a day or two."

She paused, and then exhaled slowly in choppy breaths, like she was sobbing. Nick heard the emotion in her voice as she released what had been building up inside her for a long time. "I'm sorry... it's just been hard..."

"That's okay. Love you, sis. I'll be there Saturday."

They exchanged goodbyes and he hung up. He needed to be there. He wanted to make her proud of him again.

He wanted to make the people at his job tomorrow proud of him. And maybe he would get the chance to make Melanie proud of him.

Nick was determined to learn the lessons and ask himself better questions and see what happened in his life when he chose to be a winning teammate.

He had an idea, and began to look around the apartment for something.

Jack and Rich had not hung any of his pictures, so he didn't know where they were.

A few minutes later, Nick had found the collection of frames and taken one of the nicer ones into his hands. He flipped it over, removed the back, and took out the 8 x 10 picture of him and his ex-girlfriend at dinner.

Then he walked over to the granite kitchen countertop where he had left the list of commandments, grabbed it, and placed it inside the frame. He closed the back, flipped it over, and admired his handiwork.

Tomorrow it would be hanging on his bedroom wall.

But for now, he just read the list again and thought back to each of the interactions and conversations that he had experienced over the last two days.

Those people had provided him the most

important education of his life.

He had spent too long being normal.

Tomorrow he would be different.

Appendix

apply the message with useful resources

Two weeks after he had completed the most interesting road trip of his life, Nick sat down to write and send his coach this email:

Coach Watkins —

What an incredible experience. While I regret that I didn't read or appreciate the list that you shared with me back in high school, I wanted to thank you for all you have done to help me be a better man, both on and off the court.

I may be a slow learner, but I learned much more than I thought I needed to only a few days ago. I even made a poster with the 10 Commandments of Winning Teammates, and have it framed on the wall in my new apartment!

Also, I took the time to put together a few charts that I thought would be useful for helping me to apply the ideas on the list and turn them into daily behaviors that will help me to inspire and influence the people that I interact with.

I have attached a digital copy of an application guide to help me stay focused on the ten lessons, and you can print it off and make copies and share it with other players and people that you have shared the list with. Just as Ben Franklin used a chart to track his attention to his thirteen virtues, I know that the charts I have created will help myself and others to be more disciplined and intentional about being a winning teammate.

You can download a copy of the charts for free from the website I created to share your list of lessons with other people.

The website is:

www.winningteammate.com

If you want a reproduction of the list on a scroll, or if you want a big 18 x 24 size poster of the list to hang on a wall somewhere, you can order them there online, too - but they actually cost a few dollars to make!

I know now that, on a team, even when your efforts aren't visible… your efforts are still valuable. And if I want a better team, I need to be different. I need to be a winning teammate.

And, just so you know, the question you had me ask others is one that I have thought a lot about myself.

That is why I am writing this letter to you.

I have been blind to the many deposits that others have made into my life and unaware of how much more of an impact I could have on those around me.

I want you to know that I truly appreciate your belief in me.

Thanks for being patient and allowing me to eventually discover and realize the importance of the gift you shared.

And I want you to know that this isn't the only letter I will be writing.

In the spirit of commandment number three, I am going to write a letter to the people who have been winning teammates in my life. They need to know that what they did — that what they still do each day — really matters.

And maybe someday I'll do enough to earn a letter like that myself...

Sincerely,
Nick Turner

ABOUT THE AUTHOR

Sean Glaze is an author, engaging teamwork speaker, and fun team building facilitator who inspires people to have fun laughing together so they can have more success working together.

As a successful basketball coach and educator for over 20 years, Sean gained valuable insights into how to develop winning teams - and founded Great Results Teambuilding to share those lessons…

Today, he travels around the country delivering interactive team building events and entertaining keynotes that transform employees into winning teammates!

Also by Sean

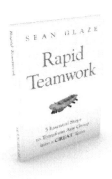

Rapid Teamwork tells the story of Greg Sharpe, a manager that readers can easily relate to. Greg's team has been underachieving and struggling with a few issues – but as a leader, he is unsure how to transform his group into a cohesive team.

What he and his executive team experience during an unusual rafting retreat is a series of lessons on how to become a more productive team quickly – creating a stronger, more unified workforce.

The Unexpected Leader is a parable that illustrates the importance of leading from where you are, regardless of title. It follows Matthew, a high school athlete, as he learns the power of vision, the impact of his words, and the influence that one person can have on their team.

This is a story that shares five steps that will inspire individuals to step up and lead during difficulty or change with intention and enthusiasm.

Made in the USA
Lexington, KY
14 July 2017